Project Management
Maturity Model

Second Edition

CENTER FOR BUSINESS PRACTICES

Editor
James S. Pennypacker
Director
Center for Business Practices
Havertown, Pennsylvania

Optimizing Human Capital with a Strategic Project Office: Select, Train, Measure, and Reward People for Organization Success, J. Kent Crawford and Jeannette Cabanis-Brewin

The Strategic Project Office: A Guide to Improving Organizational Performance, J. Kent Crawford

Managing Multiple Projects: Planning, Scheduling, and Allocating Resources for Competitive Advantage, James S. Pennypacker and Lowell Dye

The Superior Project Organization: Global Competency Standards and Best Practices, Frank Toney

The Superior Project Manager: Global Competency Standards and Best Practices, Frank Toney

Effective Opportunity Management for Projects: Exploiting Positive Risk, David Hillson

ADDITIONAL VOLUMES IN PREPARATION

Project Management
Maturity Model

Second Edition

J. Kent Crawford

Auerbach Publications
Taylor & Francis Group
Boca Raton   New York

Auerbach Publications is an imprint of the
Taylor & Francis Group, an informa business

Auerbach Publications
Taylor & Francis Group
6000 Broken Sound Parkway NW, Suite 300
Boca Raton, FL 33487-2742

© 2007 by Taylor & Francis Group, LLC
Auerbach is an imprint of Taylor & Francis Group, an Informa business

No claim to original U.S. Government works
Printed in the United States of America on acid-free paper
10 9 8 7 6 5 4 3 2 1

International Standard Book Number-10: 0-8493-7945-8 (Hardcover)
International Standard Book Number-13: 978-0-8493-7945-1 (Hardcover)

Visit the Taylor & Francis Web site at
http://www.taylorandfrancis.com

and the Auerbach Web site at
http://www.auerbach-publications.com

CONTENTS

SERIES INTRODUCTION

THE ORGANIZATIONAL ENVIRONMENT needed for project success is ultimately created by management. The way managers define, structure, and act toward projects is critical to their success or failure, and consequently the success or failure of the organization. An effective project management culture is essential for effective project management.

This Center for Business Practices series of books is designed to help you develop an effective project management culture in your organization. The series presents the best thinking of some of the world's leading project management professionals, who identify a broad spectrum of best practices for you to consider and then to implement in your own organizations. Written with the working practitioner in mind, the series provides "must have" information on the knowledge, skills, tools, and techniques used in superior project management organizations.

A culture is a shared set of beliefs, values, and expectations. This culture is embodied in your organization's policies, practices, procedures, and routines. Effective cultural change occurs and will be sustained only by altering (or in some cases creating) these everyday policies, practices, procedures, and routines in order to impact the beliefs and values that guide employee actions. We can affect the culture by changing the work climate, by establishing and implementing project management methodology, by training to that methodology, and by reinforcing and rewarding the changed behavior that results. The Center for Business

Practices series focuses on helping you accomplish that cultural change.

Having an effective project management culture involves more than implementing the science of project management, however — it involves the art of applying project management skill. It also involves the organizational changes that truly integrate this management philosophy. These changes are sometimes structural, but they always involve a new approach to managing a business: projects are a natural outgrowth of the organization's mission. They are the way in which the organization puts in place the processes that carry out the mission. They are the way in which changes will be effected that enable the organization to effectively compete in the marketplace.

We hope this Center for Business Practices series will help you and your organization excel in today's rapidly changing business world.

James S. Pennypacker
Director, Center for Business Practices
Series Editor

ACKNOWLEDGMENTS

I<small>T</small> <small>IS</small> <small>WITH</small> great pride I recognize the work of our many associates in Project Management Solutions, Inc. Over several years, our consultants provided the best of business practices for our first edition of Project Management Maturity Model. This second edition of Project Management Maturity Model has incorporated refinements from over four years of real-world experience with many of the world's leading organizations. I want to say "thank you" to each of the consultants of PM Solutions who have used the Project Management Maturity Model to measure organizational maturity, recommend cultural change improvements, and implement the intricacies of PMMM for our clients. Your work enabled the fine-tuning we are now able to share here in the second edition of our Project Management Maturity Model.

This edition would not have been published without the careful and thoughtful work of Jim Pennypacker, Director of the Center for Business Practices, and Jeannette Cabanis-Brewin, our Editor. Jim and Jeannette's tireless efforts in research, manuscript rewrites, editorial comments, and publishing have made possible this second edition of the Project Management Maturity Model.

Thanks to you, the reader, for your interest in project management and your eagerness to learn from the many years of experience represented in this book. By building a successful project management culture in your organization, you continue to develop and expand the world's most dynamic and growing profession.

J. Kent Crawford
CEO, PM Solutions

INTRODUCTION

PROJECT MANAGEMENT SOLUTIONS, INC. is a management
consulting, training, and research firm dedicated to helping
companies optimize business performance and successfully
execute their strategies through project management
improvement initiatives. Core services include project
portfolio management, project staffing/outsourcing,
organizational project management maturity assessments,
process and methodology development, project office
deployment and enhancement, project management
technology integration, value measurement, and corporate
training delivered through the PM College®.

A cornerstone product of PM Solutions has been its
Project Management Maturity Model. This model has
contributed to widespread success in assisting organizations
in improving their project management processes. The model
has been used to baseline project management practices
industry-wide, becoming the industry standard in measuring
project management maturity. This book describes the model
in full and provides you with a comprehensive tool to help
you improve your organization's project management
practices. The second edition has been revised to incorporate
changes based on revisions made to the Project Management
Institute's *A Guide to the Project Management Body of
Knowledge Third Edition (PMBOK® Guide)* and also includes
our new Project Portfolio Management Maturity Model.

PM Solutions Project Management Maturity Model
provides your organization with a conceptual framework
within which specific project management processes can be
optimized to efficiently improve the capability of your

organization. The Project Management Maturity Model provides best practices to help you to:

- determine the maturity of your organization's project management processes
- map out a logical path to improve your organization's processes
- set priorities for short-term process improvement actions
- discern the need for a project office, and assess where it fits in your organizational structure
- track progress against your project management improvement plan
- build a culture of project management excellence.

By focusing on specific processes, your organization can best leverage the resources for their improvement activities while rallying the organization around specific goals. A project management maturity model can be a roadmap showing an organization how it can systematically move to more mature levels of performance and do it in more effective and efficient ways. After an objective assessment, your organization can set its goals for increasing the capability of its processes. The ultimate goal of this book is to help you improve the capability of your organization's project management processes.

How This Book is Organized

Chapter 1 describes project management maturity and offers a brief description of the PM Solutions Project Management Maturity Model. The chapter also describes the process of assessing your organization using this model, and provides best practices for using an assessment.

Chapters 2 through 11 are the heart of the Project Management Maturity Model. Chapter 2 defines the levels of

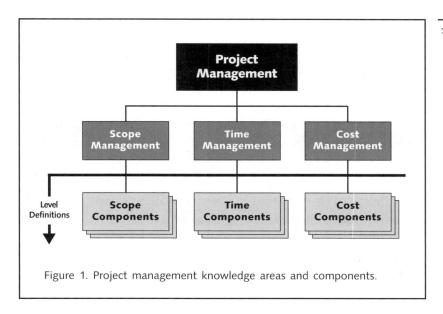

Figure 1. Project management knowledge areas and components.

project management maturity (from Level 1 through Level 5). The following chapters are based on the nine project management knowledge areas specified in the Project Management Institute's standard, *A Guide to the Project Management Body of Knowledge Third Edition (PMBOK® Guide)*. In these chapters, each knowledge area is defined at each level of maturity. In order to provide as complete a definition as possible, these knowledge areas have been broken down into their specific components (along with the additional special-interest subcomponent areas mentioned earlier). Then progressive maturity is described, level by level, for each component (see Figure 1). So Chapters 3–11 are organized as follows:

- *PMBOK® Guide* Knowledge Area (chapter title)
- General description
- Components of maturity
- Maturity level characteristics (for Levels 1–5)
- Description of component qualities in each level

Note: Definitions of component maturity are *grouped by level* within knowledge area. Achievement of a given knowledge area level by an organization is *cumulative* — that is, for each succeeding PMMM level, the assumption is that all criteria for the preceding levels for that knowledge area are being (or have been) fulfilled. So Level 5, for example, assumes that Levels 1–4 are being fulfilled, plus Level 5.

Finally, the appendices provide a checklist for self-assessing your organization's project management maturity, a summary of the changes made to the second edition based on revisions in the Project Management Institute's *A Guide to the Project Management Body of Knowledge Third Edition (PMBOK® Guide)*, and PM Solutions' Project Portfolio Management Maturity Model.

CHAPTER 1

Describing Project Management Maturity

UNTIL JUST A few years ago, the concept of "maturity" was seldom used to describe the state of an organization's effectiveness at performing certain tasks. Today, we find this maturity concept being used increasingly to map out logical ways to improve an organization's services — particularly across the software industry. Why has this evolved in this industry — why not in other areas? And why is this of interest to the project management profession? The answer to both of these questions rests in the underlying complexities that go into the successful completion of a project — software development or otherwise.

Looking at the software engineering industry, where the existing maturity models originated, it is easy to see that there are many ways to approach the resolution of any single software problem. Software development efforts typically include many more variables, unknowns, and intangibles than we would consider "normal" for a project in many other industries. Because of this complexity, the expected result of a particular software project may be more dependent on the "star" developer in a company than anything else. Unfortunately, star developers go away, and, when they do, or the projects get so large and complex that the developer's influence on them is no longer dominant, the variation in project results becomes great and leads to inevitable frustration and disappointment. Obtaining predictable results becomes a real challenge. Hence the extensive, government-funded research into how to evolve and measure an organization's effectiveness at developing software, which resulted in the Software Engineering Institute's first Capability Maturity Model. However, as we have seen through repeated use of this model in assessments, even getting organizations to the "repeatable results" level can be challenging, never mind moving toward optimization of processes.

It is logical that those of us in the project management arena learn from the efforts to improve effectiveness in the software industry. Applying project management concepts in *any* organization has many similarities to the complexities and intangibles of software development. Obtaining consistent results in any project environment involves understanding and measuring as many variables as those that exist in the software development industry. We have all seen the results of heroic efforts from project managers — those that rise above the processes and systems that support them. Take this single project manager (just like the single "star" developer in the software environment) out of the picture, and there goes the ability to ensure success. Hence the need to look at an organization's "complete" picture of project management effectiveness, or project management maturity.

Project Management Maturity Model

In organizations where we have done assessments, we have seen that the evolution of project management typically lags behind development of other capabilities within a company. It isn't until the need for project management becomes critical that organizations pay attention to improving the project management skills within their organization. This lack of foresight frequently creates an environment where the project management systems and infrastructure are not in place to support the needs of the practicing project management community. Eventually, it becomes necessary to start taking a proactive look at the infrastructure necessary to progress in project management capability. In short, the need becomes so great that the organization must respond to growing business pressures. Often, this happens when executive management decides to take proactive action — but the question is: action in what direction, and to what end?

There are a great number of interrelated challenges to deal with in improving an organization's infrastructure: project managers aren't getting the information they need to manage effectively; management is not getting accurate forecasts of completion data; there is inconsistent understanding of expectations, etc. This is often where the value of a maturity assessment comes into play. Any model selected to measure project management maturity must point out a logical path for progressive development. It may not be so important to know you are a Level 2 organization, but rather what specific actions you will be implementing to move the organization forward. What is most important is that the organization has a vision and is moving to improve the capability of project management with very targeted efforts. Improving project management is a series of smaller steps, not giant leaps, and many organizations will never need to realize Level 5 in maturity. Many organizations will achieve significant benefit by reaching the repeatable process level

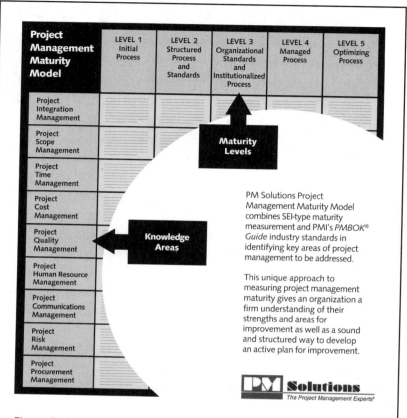

Project Management Maturity Model	LEVEL 1 Initial Process	LEVEL 2 Structured Process and Standards	LEVEL 3 Organizational Standards and Institutionalized Process	LEVEL 4 Managed Process	LEVEL 5 Optimizing Process
Project Integration Management					
Project Scope Management					
Project Time Management					
Project Cost Management					
Project Quality Management					
Project Human Resource Management					
Project Communications Management					
Project Risk Management					
Project Procurement Management					

Maturity Levels

Knowledge Areas

PM Solutions Project Management Maturity Model combines SEI-type maturity measurement and PMI's *PMBOK® Guide* industry standards in identifying key areas of project management to be addressed.

This unique approach to measuring project management maturity gives an organization a firm understanding of their strengths and areas for improvement as well as a sound and structured way to develop an active plan for improvement.

PM Solutions
The Project Management Experts

Figure 2. PM Solutions' Project Management Maturity Model utilizes the *PMBOK® Guide*'s knowledge areas and the Software Engineering Institute's five levels of maturity.

area. In effect, a good model for the measurement of project management maturity creates a strategic plan for moving project management forward in an organization.

Model Description

Key Attributes of the Knowledge Areas

The Project Management Institute's *A Guide to the Project Management Body of Knowledge (PMBOK® Guide)* is an excellent point of reference for starting an examination of project management capability. It is already an accepted standard, and there is a great deal of "best practices" information in existence around the knowledge areas outlined in the document. Unfortunately, this is a huge mass of knowledge to deal with. Measuring an organization's effectiveness in any one of the areas requires that the area be broken down further into major components that relate that area to the successful implementation of project management.

The model that PM Solutions has developed utilizes the *PMBOK® Guide*'s nine knowledge areas and is patterned after the SEI's Capability Maturity Models. The model has five distinct levels of maturity and examines an organization's implementation across the nine project management knowledge areas (see Figure 2). The five levels, similar to those in the SEI models, are described below. Each of the levels represents a discrete organizational capability based on the summary-level characteristics.

Levels of Project Management Maturity

Level 1
Initial Process

- Ad hoc processes
- Management awareness

Level 2
Structured Process and Standards

- Basic processes; not standard on all projects; used on large, highly visible projects
- Management supports and encourages use
- Mix of intermediate and summary-level information
- Estimates, schedules based on expert knowledge and generic tools
- Mostly a project-centric focus

6

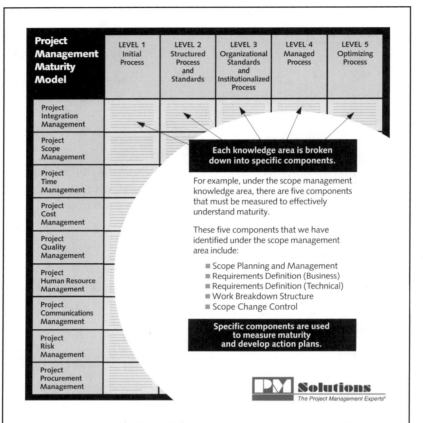

Figure 3. Because the knowledge requirement is very large within each of the *PMBOK® Guide*'s knowledge areas, it was necessary to break down each of the nine areas into key components.

Level 3

Organizational Standards and Institutionalized Process

- All processes, standard for all projects, repeatable
- Management has institutionalized processes
- Summary and detailed information
- Baseline and informal collection of actuals
- Estimates, schedules may be based on industry standards and organizational specifics

- More of an organizational focus
- Informal analysis of project performance

Level 4
Managed Process

- Processes integrated with corporate processes
- Management mandates compliance
- Management takes an organizational entity view
- Solid analysis of project performance
- Estimates, schedules are normally based on organization specifics
- Management uses data to make decisions

Level 5
Optimizing Process

- Processes to measure project effectiveness and efficiency
- Processes in place to improve project performance
- Management focuses on continuous improvement

General Component Description

As mentioned previously, because the knowledge requirement is very large within each of the *PMBOK® Guide*'s knowledge areas, it was necessary to break down each of the nine areas into key components (see Figure 3). This is where the real measurement of maturity takes place. For example, under the scope management knowledge area, there are five components that must be measured to effectively understand maturity. The five areas that we have identified within scope management include: scope planning and management, business requirements definition, technical requirements definition, work breakdown structure, and scope change control. These five components are examined independently to determine the adequacy of defining and controlling the project scope.

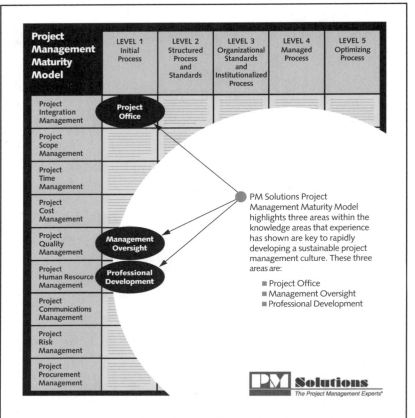

Figure 4. Three areas of significance influence the adoption of project management practices. These components are given special attention in the PM Solutions Project Management Maturity Model.

- *Scope planning and management* is the "how to" of defining the project scope. This process describes how the project team will define project scope, develop a detailed project scope statement, develop a work breakdown structure, verify the scope, and control the project scope.

- *Business requirements definition* is the assessment and development of processes, procedures, and standards relating to the collection of the business-related requirements of the project.

- *Technical requirements definition* is the assessment and development of processes, procedures, and standards relating to the collection of the technical requirements of the project.
- *Work breakdown structure* examines the formality with which an organization identifies the complete scope of work to be performed. This includes looking at the related dictionary.
- *Scope change control* looks at the process of incorporating additions, changes, and deletions to the project.

From a quick look at these five, it's easy to see that understanding the intricacies of project processes is a key element in determining project maturity. All knowledge areas must be similarly broken down.

Three Special Interest Components

There are three areas where PM Solutions has found significant influence on the adoption of project management practices. These three are project office, management oversight, and professional development. Each of these areas has special attention given it in the maturity model (see Figure 4).

Project Office. The project office makes the lives of project team members easier by supporting the team in the areas of scheduling, status reporting, project management tools, and training, among others. Some of the key items of support that the project office provides include consulting and mentoring of current staff, developing and promulgating methodologies and standards relating to project management, and serving as the central source for help in planning and managing efforts. The project office facilitates the improvement in project management maturity by being the focal point for consistent application of processes and methodologies. Often, without a project office, the project management efforts of the organization are not consistent and are not focused toward a common vision. So, the project office serves as the proverbial glue that holds the project management efforts of the organization together.

Management Oversight. Another key component in facilitating an increase in project management maturity is the amount of management oversight and involvement that key leaders of the organization have in the project management function. The bottom line here is that if management does not demonstrate active interest, then it is unlikely that project management processes will improve. If no one is holding the project manager responsible for project accomplishment and consistently measuring project performance, an unwritten signal is being sent to the project management community. Managers must make use of the data that is provided by the project management community and find ways to use this information to improve organizational performance.

Professional Development. The need for continued development of project managers is essential. Project management is itself an odd mixture of technical skills, management skills, and leadership skills that few people naturally exhibit. Most of us require continued refinement and renewal of the skills. The project management profession also continues to broaden its knowledge base — there are always new skills to learn in the project management profession.

The Five Levels of Maturity

Why SEI CMMs Are Used as the Standard

As mentioned earlier in this chapter, research into why software projects were so often completed late, over-budget, and failed to deliver what the end user really wanted resulted in the Software Engineering Capability Maturity Model (SW-CMM), a way of measuring an organization's maturity in those software engineering processes generally accepted as crucial to successful project completion. This and later Capability Maturity Models have become de facto standards for process modeling and assessing an organization's maturity in several process areas (e.g., personnel management, systems engineering). Since the CMM concept has received such widespread acceptance, it makes sense to develop a Project Management Maturity Model (PMMM) that follows the same structure.

The Key Practice Areas with the CMMs include areas familiar to those who have read the *PMBOK® Guide*: project planning, project execution and project monitoring and control. The PMMM takes those areas and further decomposes them into specific knowledge areas and the processes associated with those areas.

Notes in Measuring against the Five Levels

Too often we see the implementation of new tools or techniques as a panacea that will solve all of our problems. Maturity models can be misapplied the same way. First, there is the possibility of error in the performance of the assessment. Determining the correct level of maturity in an organization is something less than science but more than art. There are many factors that go into determining this level including individual interviews, as well as evaluating artifacts, processes, standards, knowledge, and company culture. So there is a subjective nature to determining the level of maturity, although it's unlikely that a wide margin of error will occur. It is extremely important to use an assessment tool that has been tested and proven to achieve consistent and correct results.

Additionally, the results of an assessment can be misused. An assessment should really be aimed at providing a path forward for the organization in improving its project management capabilities. Typically, organizations start with a baseline assessment of their current situation. This is accomplished by performing a comprehensive assessment evaluating all areas where project management has an influence. From here, a periodic, abbreviated assessment can indicate where progress is being made in the application of project management methodologies. The baseline assessment enables an organization to identify those areas that will provide the greatest return on investment and will show where immediate actions will have an impact.

There is a great difference between each of the five levels; organizations should strive to fill in the pockets that are weak while advancing those that will provide benefit. Striving to increase the maturity level just for the sake of having a higher level is an unwise use of the tool. It is also recommended that an organization attempt to maintain a close relationship of levels across the various knowledge areas. It has been our experience that the benefits associated with achieving a Level 5 maturity in one knowledge area may be erased if the other knowledge areas are all at Level 2 maturity.

So, what takes place during a maturity assessment? Any thorough assessment has the following four ingredients (at a minimum):

• Personal and/or group interviews
• Artifact collection and evaluation
• Widespread survey input
• Benchmark comparison to established standards.

There is little substitute for the sense of discipline, understanding, and buy-in that can be obtained from a direct personal interview with a project management practitioner. This is a necessary element of an assessment to uncover the degree to which policy is put into practice. Coupled with this is the collection of evidence (artifacts) supporting the implementation of project management — are all the documents required by policy complete, are they of high quality, etc.? Third, are the concepts of project management understood and utilized by the major population that should have knowledge about the policies and procedures? What is the general view of the project management requirements, etc.? Last, synthesizing the data and comparing this information against an established standard that is logical, sound, and clear to provide a path forward is essential. Any assessment that does not consist of at least these elements may leave an organization wondering where the benefit lies with the process.

Using the Results of an Assessment

The real value in performing an assessment comes into play across several areas. Several of these areas are listed in the paragraphs below.

Culture Change

One of the more difficult and most important aspects of instilling project management discipline in an organization is changing the behavior and habits of the people doing the work. Through the process of performing an assessment, the work products and process that people are using will be evaluated and compared to some best-practice scenarios. As this process takes place, staff members have the opportunity to identify with the logic in the new processes and gain an initial understanding of what project management has to offer. Thus culture change starts to take place with the start of the initial assessment. Staff members begin to realize that they need to think differently than they have in the past. In many cases, individuals already know that change is necessary. They're just not sure in what direction change should occur. During the interviews performed during an assessment some indication of that direction is given to the staff members.

Another good avenue for starting cultural change is the communication of a vision. The results of the assessment provide a clear path and tangible actions that can be implemented for the company to move forward. This information can be communicated across the company in an easily understood fashion to start people thinking in new directions. By using the assessment information (which is based on information provided by all levels of employees), staff members become a part of the plan to promote change or at least feel they have an understanding of where the future for the company lies. This is one starting point to generate interest and enthusiasm to improve project management.

Project Office Implementation

The assessment can help answer another important question: What is the appropriate level of the organization at which to implement a project office? The project office, by definition, is the center of excellence for project management. Less clear is the level of the organization at which the center should exist. This will depend on the degree of maturity that exists within the rest of the organization. More mature organizations typically have a project office at higher levels of the organization than those that are just starting in the project management progression. Normally, what we see is that organizations who have fairly well-established processes for project management already have competently functioning project offices at Level I (see Figure 5) and are working on

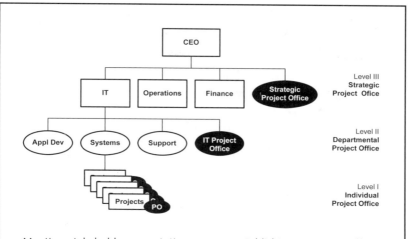

Meeting stakeholder expectations means establishing a project office at the correct level in an organization.

Level I. An Individual Project Office where individual project practices and skills are developed and refined

Level II. A Departmental Project Office builds on a Level I PMO by adding multi-project capabilities such as interproject dependencies and departmental resource management

Level III. An Enterprise Project Office further adds the dimensions of enterprise level integration and roll-up of data, as well as portfolio analysis and decision making

Figure 5. Levels of a project office.

their implementation of a Level II project office. Those organizations that are very mature will likely be working on enterprise-level project offices. In each case, the assessment will reveal the actions necessary to ensure success in the next step of the project office implementation. In all of the above cases, it will become evident that the ownership for improving project management within the organization must rest within a centralized location — usually the project office.

Repeated/Periodic Use as a Progress and Effectiveness Tool

We find many of our clients periodically ask themselves: "Are we making a difference?" or "Are we advancing the project management capability in the right areas, and in general?" Recurring use of the assessment can show the progress that the project office is making toward helping the organization reach its goals. This can become a part of the metrics that are used to measure success of a project office on a recurring basis. If the project office owns the project management capability improvement action, then the results of the assessment can be attributed to the actions taken by the project office to improve project management capability. It is possible to use these measures as the basis of incentive rewards.

Periodic assessments ensure improvements are taking root, reinforcing adoption of new ways. Essentially, repeated assessments can be used to track progress against the project management deployment plan that would be developed as a result of the initial assessment.

Target Six-Month Improvement Goals

We often find that organizations want to use the assessment as a tool to identify specific areas of improvement that become goals for the next incremental period of time. They then tackle one area, one level, at a time. This allows organizations to show improvements over a 6–12 month period so that the improvement sponsors see a solid return on investment (ROI). Small victories provide an opportunity to cheer for successes and reevaluate specific direction while reenergizing staff members. These are important "peg points" that allow organizations to see how much they've learned, plan for what they didn't know in the first planning session, and adapt/adjust direction for the next short-term (6 months) initiative.

Another value of the short-term reassessment is that it provides a tool to communicate success and meeting milestones to executives and management. Leadership sometimes has a fairly short-range memory, and commitment to change initiative budgets can waiver with time.

Setting Your Maturity Goals

Is Level 5 for Everyone?

Level 5 maturity is not for everyone. Each organization needs to determine the minimum level of maturity at which the desired value, be it measured by ROI in terms of dollars or improvements in customer satisfaction, return on investment is achieved and then determine the value associated with achieving the next level. It is important to realize that these levels are evolutionary steps. We recommend that our clients establish an incremental improvement program with specific focus and measurable goals that allow their organization to realize some benefits within a short period of time. We recommend 6-month increments, whenever possible.

We have also found it beneficial to maintain project management maturity in synch with other corporate process maturity, including financial management, software engineering, etc. For instance, implementing mature project management processes such as earned value tracking is meaningless if the organization has not implemented time reporting processes. Experience shows that advancing project management practices far ahead of other corporate processes can cause turmoil and mistrust.

Assessing Your Level

So, how do you determine where you are currently? There are two kinds of assessments that can be conducted. The first assessment approach is the *independent assessment*. Project management experts, possessing a strong blend of project controls, organizational structure, project management, professional development, and management skills, plus an in-depth understanding of the PMMM, would conduct the assessment. Using a prescribed set of tools and processes (like PM Solutions' PMMM Assessment and HealthCheck^{SM}), these experts would determine your organization's maturity levels in the various knowledge areas and present the results to your management team. The management team and the assessors would then work together to develop your improvement plan. This independent approach is the preferred method when an external "expert voice" is needed to communicate to senior executives.

The second assessment approach is a *facilitated assessment*. A small team of experienced assessors would team with representatives from your staff to conduct a self-assessment. Following the same procedures that an independent assessment would follow, this team of individuals would determine your organization's maturity levels in the various knowledge areas. The team would then work with your management staff to develop an improvement plan to achieve your desired maturity level. The primary challenge in the self-assessment approach is maintaining the confidentiality of individual findings. The assessment fact-finding activities include staff interviews. The quality of the information provided in these interviews can be skewed if staff members are not comfortable sharing negative information with other staff members. The self-assessment approach can also suffer from an inherent bias toward a higher level of maturity; no one likes to hear they are at Level 1 maturity.

Conclusion

The benefits of a structured assessment of project management maturity lie in setting direction, prioritizing actions, and beginning cultural change rather than in understanding the current level at which an organization is performing. The emphasis is on "structured." It is important that the assessment itself be repeatable, provide consistent measurements and results, and provide for some degree of benchmarking with other organizations. This provides the basis for any assessment to be utilized as a "checkup" tool to measure progress, and to identify the next logical steps forward. Like it or not, maturity assessments may be here to stay in this complex project management world we live in — not too distant or different from the software development world and SEI's maturity models.

Project Management
Maturity Model

CHAPTER 2

Definitions of Maturity Levels

THE LEVELS IN the PM Solutions Project Management Maturity Model are as follows:

Level 1: Initial Process

Although there is a recognition that there are project management processes, there are no established practices or standards, and individual project managers are not held to specific accountability by any process standards. Documentation is loose and ad hoc. Management understands the definition of a project, that there are accepted processes, and is aware of the need for project management. Metrics are informally collected on an ad hoc basis.

Level 2: Structured Process and Standards

Many project management processes exist in the organization, but they are not considered an organizational standard. Documentation exists on these basic processes. Management supports the implementation of project management, but there is neither consistent understanding, involvement, nor organizational mandate to comply for all projects.

Functional management is involved in the project management of larger, more visible projects, and these are typically executed in a systematic fashion. There are basic metrics to track project cost, schedule, and technical performance, although data may be collected/correlated manually. Information available for managing the project is often a mix between summary-level data and detail-level data.

Level 3: Organizational Standards and Institutionalized Process

All project management processes are in place and established as organizational standards. These processes involve clients and internal customers as active and integral members of the project team. Nearly all projects use these processes with minimal exception — management has institutionalized the processes and standards with formal documentation existing on all processes and standards. Management is regularly involved in input and approval of key decisions and documents and in key project issues. The project management processes are typically automated. Each project is evaluated and managed in light of other projects.

Important note: At Level 3, the processes must become tailorable to the characteristics of each project. An organization cannot blindly apply all processes equally to all projects. Consideration must be given to the differences between projects. The important thing is to note how the processes are tailored — that is, is there a process to customize the implementation of applicable processes/policies to a particular project?

Level 4: **Managed Process**

Projects are managed with consideration as to how the project performed in the past and what is expected for the future. Management uses efficiency and effectiveness metrics to make decisions regarding the project and understands the impacts on other projects. All projects, changes, and issues are evaluated based upon metrics from cost estimates, baseline estimates, and earned value calculations. Project information is integrated with other corporate systems to optimize business decisions. Processes and standards are documented and in place to support the practice of using such metrics to make project decisions. Management clearly understands its role in the project management process and executes it well, managing at the right level, and clearly differentiating management styles and project management requirements for different sizes/complexities of projects. Project management processes, standards, and supporting systems are integrated with other corporate processes and systems.

Level 5: **Optimizing Process**

Processes are in place and actively used to improve project management activities. Lessons learned are regularly examined and used to improve project management processes, standards, and documentation. Management and the organization are focused not only on effectively managing projects but also on continuous improvement. The metrics collected during project execution are used not only to understand the performance of a project but also for making organizational management decisions for the future.

CHAPTER 3

Project Integration Management

THE PURPOSE OF project integration management is to (1) initiate the project; (2) coordinate project activities and integrate all efforts into a project management plan; (3) integrate, analyze, and report the project results in carrying out the project management plan; (4) control changes to the baseline plan; (5) collect, integrate, and organize project information in a project information system; and (6) close the project in an orderly and disciplined fashion.

Components

Initiation and Scope Definition

Initiation and scope definition involves the processes in place for the formal authorization of a project and the definition of project scope, assumptions, and constraints. Are they formal or informal? Do these processes cause the project scope to be well defined? Are projects always begun with a project charter? Are scope, assumptions, and constraints regularly tracked for projects?

28 Deliverables Identification

Deliverables identification is the process established to identify the resultant work products, or project deliverables, that the project is to have produced upon its successful completion. Stakeholder involvement is described (client, management, etc.), and mapping to the original business request is covered.

Project Management Plan Development

Project management plan development integrates planning information from the other knowledge areas to create a project management plan. The project management plan provides a roadmap for project execution and is the integration vehicle that ensures all project management areas are addressed, developed, and managed within the context of the project. The outcome of this component is a project management plan.

Project Management Plan Execution

Project management plan execution is performing the work by carrying out the project management plan. During project execution, work progress is examined from the perspective of each knowledge area (i.e., scope, time, cost, quality, etc.). The status and performance of the project from the perspective of each knowledge area is consolidated and integrated into progress reports. The main product of this component is information on the work results, usually depicted in project status and performance reports.

Change Control

Integrated change control addresses managing the project baseline. Integrated change control includes implementing a change control system (to include configuration management), identifying and assessing changes to the baseline, coordinating the changes across the knowledge areas, managing the authorized changes, informing stakeholders, and identifying corrective actions. The main products from this component include change requests, updates to the project plan, corrective actions, and lessons learned.

Project Closure

Project closure includes those processes associated with the orderly closure of a project, be the project completed or cancelled. This process involves all activities to insure contractual obligations are met, requirements have been fulfilled, deliverables accepted by the client, and contractual and administrative closure procedures have been performed. Furthermore, organizational knowledge and project artifacts are collected and preserved for learning purposes and potential re-use in other projects.

Project closure includes actions involved with vendor management during contract performance, acceptance by the client, payment for services, and close-out activities. The purpose is to assure that the seller performs in accordance with the terms of the contract and receives proper reimbursement (in both quantity and timing).

Project Information System

This component covers the project's information system that collects, integrates, and organizes project-related information, tools, processes, and procedures across the knowledge areas. The main product of this component is information about the project that is readily accessible to all stakeholders. Note, this includes manual-based systems.

Special Interest Component — Project Office

The project office is an "office" staffed by project management professionals who serve their organization's project management needs. In particular, this office provides project management support services, provides project management consulting/mentoring, develops and maintains project management methodologies/standards, trains project managers within the organization, and supplies project managers for major project initiatives.

The project office assists project teams by providing support in the areas of project scheduling, report production and distribution, operation of project management software, maintenance of the visibility room, and maintenance of the project workbook. The types of integration activities that can reasonably be expected from a project office include:

Consulting/Mentoring

As organizations mature in project management, the project office satisfies an increasing need for internal project management consultants. These people will provide the organization with the expert insights it needs to execute projects effectively.

Processes/Standards

The project office is the unit within the organization that develops and promulgates common methodologies and standards relating to project management.

Training

The project office trains project managers, team members, and clients regarding project management principles, tools, and techniques. Both training materials and instructors originate in the project office.

Project Management

The project office can house a group of professional project managers who can be assigned to carry out the organization's projects.

Project Management Software Tools

As the project office matures it becomes the focal point in the organization for software tools supporting the project management effort.

<u>Level 1</u>
Initial Process

There is recognition of the need for accepted processes, but there are no established practices or standards. Individual teams or parts of the organization may have their own way of doing things in an ad hoc, informal fashion. Documentation of the processes is loose and makes it difficult to repeat the activities elsewhere. Management is aware of the importance of project integration on an ad hoc basis and asks for information on work results.

Initiation and Scope Definition

Projects are initiated informally, perhaps even verbally, by someone in management. Generally a statement of scope is prepared on a project. However, the format and content of this statement are ad hoc — that is, there are no standards for such, and each one looks different.

Deliverables Identification

Deliverables are documented only by naming them (perhaps a bulleted list).

Project Management Plan Development

Some project managers have developed individual versions of project management plans on an ad hoc basis; thus each plan looks different with varying amounts of content and levels of detail. If a project management plan exists, it may include a scope statement and work breakdown structure (WBS) that consists of a basic set of milestones and, occasionally, deliverables. The plan may include independent milestones and key resource requirements.

Project Management Plan Execution

Assignment of work is informal and is typically through verbal communications. The information on work results is developed on an ad hoc basis, in response to specific requests.

Change Control

Changes are communicated in an ad hoc manner to the project manager and, in some cases, directly to the team without project manager awareness/ involvement. The project manager sometimes documents them. There is no documented change control process and individual project teams are applying their own approach to managing and controlling change. Changes are unequally managed and, in many cases, not monitored. Configuration control of deliverables is loosely managed and controlled, if at all.

Project Closure

Final product or service is delivered informally, with or without customer acceptance. No procedures exist for dispersion of project team or collection of project data. Contracts for projects are loosely managed with minimal reporting requirements delineated within the contract. In large part, vendors/contractors are managed to end dates only. There are no procedures for shutting down a project that has been cancelled.

Project Information System

There is no system that collects, integrates, and organizes project-related information tools, processes, and procedures across knowledge areas. Each project manager uses whatever system she or he desires.

Project Office

An informal project office *may* exist that generally consists of one or two people who have an interest in bringing project management standards to the organization and are acknowledged as successful project managers. This is a very basic project office — basically in name only. More often, a project office does not exist at all.

Project Support
Assistance is available from the project office to project teams on scheduling of projects.

Consulting/Mentoring
No help is available within the organization.

Processes/Standards
Each project manager manages his or her project in the manner he or she desires.

Training
No formalized training is available. If training is requested, individuals are directed to seek outside sources.

Project Management
Guidance on project management concepts may be available to individuals upon request.

Project Management Software Tools
Each project manager uses whatever scheduling tool and methodology she or he desires. There is no tool commonality in the organization.

Level 2
Structured Process and Standards

There are basic, documented processes in place for developing project plans and integrating, analyzing, and developing the reports on work results. Summary-level information is consolidated into reports. The focus is on summary status and performance reporting for the triple constraint items (scope, time, cost). Although the processes are in place, they are not considered an organizational standard. Management supports the efforts and is involved on large, highly visible projects.

Initiation and Scope Definition

There is a clearly defined and documented process describing the preparation of project charters and scope statements, which is enforced by organizational management for larger, more visible projects. Projects are consistently started with the defined project charter; scope statements are consistently prepared in accordance with the defined process and format.

Deliverables Identification

There is a process in place by which key deliverables are identified and listed. There is a process in place requiring management and customer involvement in the deliverables identification/approval process.

Project Management Plan Development

The organization has a documented process for developing a project management plan. The process is mandatory for large, highly visible projects, and optional for others. At this point, the project management plan incorporates a project charter, scope statement, and top-level work breakdown structure (WBS). The plan also includes a summary-level cost estimate and schedule with major milestones. The plan includes key resource requirements and identified risks, as well as a list of key stakeholders and a communication strategy with those key individuals. The plan includes basic staff management items such as time reporting and vacation request procedures. The project management plans are updated to reflect approved scope changes from the change control process.

Project Management Plan Execution

Summary-level information on work results is developed. Both status and performance reports are produced tracking progress toward achieving scheduled milestones. Technical status information is integrated with the cost and schedule information to depict the project status. Basic metrics (such as planned budget, milestone percent complete) are collected and integrated into project performance reports.

Change Control

There is a defined and documented change control process for scope changes. For large and highly visible projects, scope changes are identified with a change request form, tracked on a change request log, are formally approved, and project plans are updated and corrective actions incorporated, if necessary. Cost and schedule changes are not yet controlled since baselines are not yet common practice nor established as an organizational standard. Functional, physical, and data configuration is documented and maintained. Large, highly visible projects are required to use the principles of change control.

Project Closure

Formal acceptance and contract closure occurs, but a standard process is not established or documented. Corrective action information and other changes are managed via the project integration management change control process, resulting in project management plan updates.

Closure information and formal acceptance is provided by way of the communication management process. Finance provides final performance numbers to the project manager. The project manager notifies the personnel assigned to the project to report back to their functional supervisors.

There is no standard process for closing down a cancelled project; however, it is generally known that the project manager maintains a file of documentation and information that had been generated by project efforts to date.

Larger, more visible projects receive more attention to close-out procedures, both administrative and contractual; smaller projects are not scrutinized.

Project Information System

There is a basic project system that collects, integrates, and organizes project-related information tools, processes, and procedures across knowledge areas for large and highly visible projects. The system may be something as simple as a central file system. There are guidelines for acceptable information systems for individual project teams, but the responsibility for selection/deployment lies with the project managers.

Project Office

A basic project office is established and recognized by upper management as having the responsibility to define the processes and standards by which projects should be managed. The individuals within the project office (sometimes a part-time responsibility) advise and offer input when asked.

Project Support
The project office assists project teams in the creation and maintenance of their project workbooks. Assistance is offered to project teams on developing scope, project scheduling, and issue and change control, upon request.

Consulting/Mentoring
On major projects the project office is asked to provide personal consulting and mentoring to project managers on project initiation and planning processes.

Processes/Standards
The project office has put in place a basic project management process; it is not considered an organizational standard, and only large or highly visible projects are using it.

Training
Basic project management concepts training is made available to project managers.

Project Management
A database of all project managers in the organization is maintained, along with their experience and skill set.

Project Management Software Tools

There is an accepted project management scheduling tool as a guideline; however, the responsibility for project management tool selection/deployment lies with the project managers.

Level 3
Organizational Standards and Institutionalized Process

Additional processes are developed and documented for creating project plans, reporting information on work results, controlling changes, and evolving the project information system. There is a coordinated effort within the organization to have a common information system set up for individual project teams. The project management processes are considered standard practice for projects. Management supports project management and is actively involved — particularly on large, visible projects. Management monitors status, performance, and changes and responds with corrective actions, as required. Systems are becoming more integrated: the project information systems are integrated with the project office. Management fully supports project integration efforts and has institutionalized the procedures and standards related to integration activities.

Initiation and Scope Definition

A statement of work is created for each project with specific definition of the work and is approved by organizational management. It is well-known policy for all projects that work does not start without an authorizing Project Charter. The project scope is regularly determined and documented by a fully integrated project team, including the business unit, technical groups, strategic groups as necessary, the client, etc. Project assumptions and constraints are clearly documented in the Preliminary Project Scope Statement.

Deliverables Identification

A Level 3 organization includes project requestor/ user involvement in a facilitated process, and complete integrated project team involvement in the process of identifying and documenting the deliverables. This process includes a deliverables dictionary, where the dictionary discusses what each deliverable is, the scope of each deliverable, the expectations of what each deliverable will achieve, the business or technical requirement/specification that each deliverable will satisfy. The process must include a documented agreement by the project sponsor (or designee) to this deliverable dictionary.

Project Management Plan Development

The project management plan development process is fully documented and implemented within the organization, and applied to all projects. The organization's process for developing project management plans incorporates management plans (procedures, processes, etc.) from cost, schedule, risk, quality, procurement, communications, and human resources (staff management and staff development). In addition to management plans for each knowledge area, project management plans will typically include specific scope, time, cost, and risk information at an appropriate level of detail. For example, the project management plans will include the project charter, scope statement, and WBS (possibly down to level three). The plan will also include cost estimates and schedule information at the level needed for visibility and control. The plan includes the cost and schedule baseline. The plan identifies key resource requirements from the staff management plan. The plan identifies risks and planned mitigation strategies, as appropriate, and includes a list of key stakeholders and the communication strategy with those key individuals. The project management plans are updated to reflect approved project changes from the change control process. Program management plans are developed for common, related projects.

Project Management Plan Execution

Summary and detail-level information on work results is integrated and analyzed, and reports are developed. Status and performance reports are produced addressing items such as technical performance of the project, time spent on project activities, and the amount of hours or dollars spent. These reports will include informal variance and performance measurement analysis. (Note: At this point, the actuals are estimated by project teams as opposed to being extracted from corporate finance/accounting systems.) Report templates may exist. The status and performance reports include information from knowledge areas such as risk, quality, human resource, and procurement management (in addition to scope, time, and cost). Metrics are collected from the knowledge areas and integrated into project performance reports.

Change Control

There is a defined and documented project change control system that incorporates the change control processes for scope, cost, and schedule, and is therefore a truly *Integrated* Change Control System. The process includes the change control form and change log. The project integrated change control system and processes are implemented and utilized by the project teams (changes are identified, assessed, coordinated, managed, stakeholders are informed, and corrective action is taken). The process is documented and repeatable, and project plan updates are consistently incorporated with corrective actions and approved changes. Baselines are established, adhered to, and managed.

Project Closure

Project reporting and deliverable acceptance formats/processes are defined and used consistently. Any changes/issues are communicated immediately via the project manager to appropriate project stakeholders. The integrated change management process is fully implemented within the project.

The users/clients are integrally involved in review of documentation and testing of the product and sign off on deliverable completion. After the customer has signed off on the acceptability of the delivered items, and all appropriate documentation has been received, the project sponsor signs off on the project acceptance document and closure actions take place.

There are standard processes for closure on all projects that dictate who is to receive communication of project closure, the type and format of financial data that is provided and to whom. Project data is captured in an established repository in specific formats established by the company.

Project team members receive project performance evaluations and are afforded the opportunity for 360° reviews.

There is a process for "shutting down" any project that is cancelled by management.

Project Information System

> There is a central project system that collects, integrates, and organizes project-related information tools, processes, and procedures across knowledge areas. The systems are becoming standardized across projects and may encompass a central file system and project workbooks. The project office provides guidance and coordinates the selection and implementation of project management systems.

Project Office

> Functions and services of the project office are defined and communicated to the organization. The project office is considered by most project managers as a reference site and an overseer of project management methodology. It is considered by organizational management as the focal point of the project management thrust for the organization. There is a comprehensive standardized project management methodology in place and project team resources are being actively trained in its usage. The project office is an accepted part of the organizational project management landscape. It is integrally involved with the project managers in the organization.

> ### Project Support
> The project office closely monitors the issue and change control systems and is consulted on crucial change (scope) decisions on large, highly visible projects. The project office monitors risk analysis on large, highly visible projects and is involved in the risk analysis and control processes on these projects. Assistance is offered on project resource and cost

estimating. The project office offers assistance to project teams in preparing project performance reports and closely monitors time reporting to projects. All support roles (schedulers, etc.) report to the line organization. The project office offers assistance to project teams upon request in preparing schedule and progress reports.

Consulting/Mentoring
The project office works closely with the project teams of major projects in the planning process. This assistance is also available to smaller projects upon request.

Processes/Standards
The project management methodology is enhanced with templates and samples for project management deliverables. The project office actively works with the project managers to ascertain the best practices for the organization; they are documented in the project management methodology. The project office provides quality standards and processes. There is a project management guide in place that provides a reference for project managers on the entire life cycle of managing a project. It integrates with the more basic process already in place and the templates/ samples in place. The project office is involved in regular quality walk-throughs and checks throughout the project life cycle

Training
Project management essentials training is considered mandatory for project managers and is made available to project team members.

Project Management

The project office is consulted for the assignment of project managers to major projects. The project office works closely with the project managers on major projects. The project office has an initial, generic resource listing (labor categories) in place for the use of project teams. Resource leveling is performed at the project level.

There is concern about balancing and scheduling key resource usage at an organizational level, but no such tools are in place, so this is done manually, if at all.

Project Management Software Tools

The project office provides guidance and coordinates the selection and implementation of project management software tools — project managers in the organization are involved in tool selection.

Level 4
Managed Process

All processes are in place, documented, and being utilized by all projects. Processes and standards are integrated with other corporate processes and systems. Integration includes incorporating project plans and program plans into organization strategic plans. In addition, the reporting process and project information system are integrated with the project office, finance/accounting, strategic planning systems, and risk management process. There is a mandate to comply with the organizational project management processes and procedures. Management takes an "organizational view" of projects. Projects are managed with consideration as to how the project performed in the past and what is expected for the future. Management uses efficiency and effectiveness metrics to make decisions regarding the project. All projects, changes, and issues are evaluated based upon metrics from cost estimates, baseline estimates, and earned value calculations. The metrics are used to understand the performance of a project during execution for making management decisions for the future.

Initiation and Scope Definition

Projects are chartered with an "organizational view." Chartering a project is an ingrained and efficient process. Scope, assumptions, constraints, and interproject dependencies are thoroughly documented and actively monitored and managed throughout the project.

Deliverables Identification

Organizational management has mandated that deliverables must be planned and delivered with a clear, consistent view to other existing functions,

systems, and active projects. The development of a
WBS is closely aligned with deliverable identification
and documentation.

Project Management Plan Development

All processes are in place, documented, and being
utilized. Project management plans and program
management plans are integrated into and support
organization strategic plans. Data from project
management plans feed into financial and other
organizational systems to complement business
execution.

Project Management Plan Execution

All processes are in place, documented, and being
utilized. The status and performance reporting process
is integrated with the project office, finance/
accounting, strategic planning systems, and risk
management systems. Formal variance and
performance measurement analysis is conducted and
reported. (Note: At this point, the actuals are extracted
from corporate finance/accounting systems.) Metrics
are collected from the knowledge areas and integrated
into project performance reports.

Change Control

All change control processes are in place,
documented, and being utilized. The project change
control process, to include configuration
management, is integrated with the organization's
control systems, monitoring programs, and risk
management process. Functional, physical, and data
configuration is consistently documented,
maintained, managed, and controlled for all projects.

Project Closure

The project manager and team are required to report progress against plan using the organization's standard project management tools and techniques. All project resources, to include vendors, are fully integrated into the project closing activities.

A process and repository exist for capture of appropriate project information and presentation/ access of historical project information for re-use in estimating, risk management, and project planning.

The organization provides resources and time in order to conduct "Sunset" or lessons learned briefings upon project closure. Project teams are recognized for their efforts.

All projects that are terminated prematurely are closed using a standard process for capturing all relevant artifacts and data. Lessons learned regarding terminated projects are also captured and reviewed.

Project Information System

The central project system collects, integrates, and organizes project-related information tools, processes, and procedures across knowledge areas. The systems are standardized across projects and are integrated with the project office and other corporate systems, as applicable. Data require minimal manual effort in moving from, and to, the project manager.

Project Office

Project management best practices are collected by functional area and maintained at the project office. Realistic management-level reporting is in place. "Ego-less" reviews of major projects are regularly done against standard methodologies and processes. Realistic resource projections are done by the project office. There are few surprises on projects.

Project Support

The project office is responsible for the organizational skill inventory database, coordination of the assignments of critical resources, organizational resource leveling, and resource projections (also involved in the requisition of additional/replacement resources). The project office provides project-level variance analyses to organizational management. They also design and produce executive dashboard management reporting on all approved projects. The project office maintains visibility rooms for all major projects, and possibly a room(s) for smaller projects to share. The project office determines the project report consolidation process for management reporting and is responsible for carrying it out on a regular cycle.

Consulting/Mentoring

There is a project audit process in place. Projects that are in trouble are immediately put into a project recovery process that is managed by the project office. A formal mentoring process is in place, whereby all project managers are mentored at some point.

Processes/Standards

The project management methodology is now a standard. All projects are expected to use these processes as their normal operating process. A central project documentation repository is in place and is actively monitored by the project office. Projects are required to utilize this repository. The project office conducts benchmarking of selected projects to ascertain estimate accuracy and improve estimating techniques.

Training

Advanced project management topics are considered mandatory for project managers — a training plan, tied into the career plan, is created for each project manager. Project management essentials training is made available to project managers. Advanced project management topics are made available to project managers. Project management essentials training is mandatory before a project manager manages a project and is suggested for all team members.

Project Management

Performance reviews of project managers are done jointly by the line organization and the project office. There is an accurate resource repository in place; the project office is responsible for maintenance of this information, which is used for organizational resource projections. The project managers report to the line organization; however, there is a dotted-line responsibility to the project office. Regular status reports go to both the line organization and the project office. There may be a small cadre of senior project managers who report to the project office. They manage the more complex, visible projects for the organization. The project office provides input to the line manager for the project manager's performance review. The project office is responsible for the acquisition and updating of resource information (especially for key resources), and this process has begun. The project office manually ties in resource leveling to resource availability at an organizational level. The project office is responsible for integrating project performance reports into the consolidated report, which is sent into the management oversight process.

Project Management Software Tools

Since estimates are now being entered for all projects, the project office is capturing estimated and actual costs. The project office drives the selection of project management software tools, soliciting input from the line organization. The project office is responsible for deploying project management software tools. The project management software tool has resource repository information.

Level 5
Optimizing Process

Improvement procedures are in place and utilized. Lessons learned are regularly examined and used to improve documented processes.

Initiation and Scope Definition

The process of initiating a project and determining and documenting scope is regularly examined to ascertain process improvements. Experience data from a project repository are regularly used to improve upon standard templates for scoping and the development of requirements. Scope is regularly monitored carefully and projected deviations from scope are foreseen and carefully documented. They are carefully evaluated based upon value propositions (cost/time/value) before the determination is made whether or not to proceed with the deviation.

Deliverables Identification

There is full change control on deliverables. Any change is only initiated if it is fully understood and documented; management has approval at appropriate levels. The processes incorporate quality assurance techniques and quality improvement processes on an ongoing basis such that history is kept on how past projects defined and documented deliverables; this history is used to determine improvements in the process used for understanding and documenting deliverables. The decisions for any change in deliverables (that is, change to the deliverable dictionary) must be based upon a value proposition: dollar impact, time impact, some value impact. There must be metrics involved in such decisions.

54 Project Management Plan Development

An improvement process is in place to continuously improve project management plan development. Lessons learned are captured and used to improve the planning efforts. Project and program plans are used to support strategic organization decisions and decisions regarding projects. A process utilizing the project and program plans for such decisions is developed, documented, and in place. The organization has evolved to the point where the act of planning a project is clearly understood and its consumption of resources is planned as well.

Project Management Plan Execution

An improvement process is in place to continuously improve project management plan execution. Lessons learned are captured and used to improve the execution efforts. The project status and performance reports are used to understand the efficiency and effectiveness of a project during execution. The project's overall performance is used to support decisions regarding the project and organization strategy. A process utilizing the project metrics to support management decisions is developed, documented, and in place. Lessons learned are being captured.

Change Control

Project changes are included in the determination of project efficiency and effectiveness. In addition, evaluation and analysis of potential changes includes efficiency and effectiveness considerations. A process utilizing such metrics for management decisions during project execution is developed, documented, and in place. Lessons learned are being captured in a repository.

An improvement process is in place to continuously improve the project integrated change control process to include configuration management. Lessons learned are captured and used to improve the monitoring and control efforts. Historical changes on projects are examined to identify trends in change control actions and improve upon the initial project planning process.

Project Closure

Project closure processes are evaluated on a periodic basis and enhancements are continuously incorporated. The organization adheres to a high standard of project performance and quality in their products or services. Captured on large and highly visible projects are lessons learned about the project management process within the project with regard to effectiveness and efficiency (e.g., processing project information and documentation, integrated change control, and vendor management). A performance database exists to capture performance information on the project, to include vendors/contractors.

All cancelled projects undergo a review process in order to determine root causes for capture as lessons learned.

Project Information System

An improvement process is in place to continuously improve the project information system. Lessons learned are captured and used to improve the project systems. The project information systems support the collection and organization of project efficiency and effectiveness metrics. In addition, the system employed to collect, integrate, and organize project information becomes more efficient and effective.

Project Office

The project office manages the project portfolio, provides project management tools and training, and oversees scoping of projects. Project managers are significantly accountable to the project office. The project office is responsible for organization-wide resource leveling and assignment of critical resources. The project office has processes in place to capture lessons learned from projects completed, and modifies project management methodologies as a result. Projects are measured against best practices. Lessons learned are captured and applied. Project management is now thoroughly accepted as the standard practice throughout the organization.

Project Support

There is a project management help desk function available from the project office. The project office is involved in the closure process of every major project (and many smaller ones). The project office provides, as part of management reporting, full-cost tracking, including what is necessary for earned value calculations by project.

Lessons learned are captured and used. Additionally, customer satisfaction surveys of project office support are conducted and improvement areas identified and acted on.

Consulting/Mentoring

The project office staff coaches project managers in the managing of smaller projects within the organization.

The project office works closely with project managers
and business clients on business analysis and proposal
preparation for major project initiatives.

Processes/Standards
A process is in place whereby project management
methodologies are improved as better practices are
discovered. All project management methodologies,
processes, and templates/samples are available on the
Intranet. The project office maintains an internal web site.

Training
An evaluation is made at the end of every major
project to ascertain weak skill areas. This information
is used to bolster training plans for individuals on the
project and to create changes to existing training
courses (and, occasionally, new courses). A full
training program is available, leading to certification
as a Project Management Professional (PMP®). Project
management essentials training is considered
mandatory for project managers, and is suggested for
all client personnel who will be involved in projects.

Project Management
The project manager works closely with the line
organization to anticipate new programs and projects
on the horizon. There is an active program for
feedback from all parts of the organization for project
management improvements. Many project managers
in the organization report to the project office, with
dotted-line responsibility to the line organization. The
project office does performance reviews of project
managers with input from the line organization.
    Project managers are well integrated into the
client organization (although they may report to the

project office) and are considered part of the client management teams.

Resource leveling is done in an automated fashion at the organizational level.

Project Management Software Tools

On every project, part of the closure process is to review the project management software tools and their interfaces to ascertain improvements. These lessons learned are regularly integrated back into the tools/interfaces through a standard process.

The project management software tool provides earned value reporting, which the project office has made a part of the executive dashboard reporting. The resource repository is now integrated with the human resource system for the organization. The project management software tool is integrated with the corporate accounting system for budgeting and cost reporting and with the organizational procurement system for obtaining actual costs of goods and services.

CHAPTER 4

Project Scope Management

SCOPE MANAGEMENT CONSISTS of the processes required to ensure that the project includes all the work required, and only the work required, to complete the project successfully. Scope management has the components listed below.

Components

Scope Planning and Management

This covers the "how to" of defining the project scope. The Project Scope Management Plan is a planning tool describing how the project team will define project scope, develop a detailed project scope statement, develop a work breakdown structure, verify the scope, and control the scope.

Requirements Definition (Business)

This is the assessment and development of processes, procedures, and standards relating to the collection of the business-related requirements of projects.

Requirements Definition (Technical)

This is the assessment and development of processes, procedures, and standards relating to the collection of the technical requirements of projects. It has to do with how business requirements are translated into technical requirements.

Work Breakdown Structure

This covers the process for the development of a work plan, the quality, quantity, and overall sophistication of the organization's use of the WBS. Do they develop a WBS dictionary? Does the WBS form the basis for the automated plan? Is the WBS tied to the accounting system for reporting purposes?

Scope Change Control

This section covers the change management processes as they relate to project scope. It covers the regularity of use and the overall evaluation of proposed changes. Are changes really evaluated/prioritized or are they merely listed? Is the change management process tied into the issues tracking system? Is there regular follow-up and reporting? Is the change management process closely tied to the organizational management process?

Level 1
Initial Process

There is a very general statement of business requirements that is reduced to a requirements list by the project team. Documentation and management of all elements (issues, changes, etc.) is very loose and ad hoc. Although there is an awareness of the need for managing project efforts, there are no standards in the organization for project management. Management is generally aware of the scope of the initiatives, but typically is only aware to the point of definition of a few key milestones.

Scope Planning and Management

There is no Project Scope Management Plan, rather the scope is inferred through other documents and statements from management. A Project Charter or Statement of Purpose may be the only initiating documentation available.

Requirements Definition (Business)

Business requirements are only a statement of purpose—"this is what we think we need."

Requirements Definition (Technical)

Technical requirements/deliverables are documented for projects; those deliverables have some general definition of what will be produced if these deliverables are met.

Work Breakdown Structure

The WBS consists of a very basic set of identified work to be accomplished, and occasionally deliverables (may not truly be a decomposition of the project, but more of a listing). The project may have a schedule, but that schedule has no real basis in work to be performed, and there are no specific guidelines as to how the work plan or schedule should be developed.

Scope Change Control

Changes are communicated in an ad hoc manner to the project manager, who sometimes documents them. There is no documented scope change control process.

Level 2
Structured Process and Standards

There is a basic project management scope process in place. There is a process to involve management in the project scope management process, but not all management is participating in this process. Many of the projects in the organization are utilizing the standard project management process to identify and manage project scope. Organizational management is involved in project management processes on the larger, more visible projects, but there may not be consistent management involvement across all projects, nor an organizational mandate to utilize the basic project management processes on all projects. Management is supporting the project management processes and the scope management process in particular.

Scope Planning and Management

Development of a Project Scope Management Plan is accepted as part of the project management process and is used to establish some of the rules for defining and managing the project scope. Most large and visible projects develop and utilize one.

Requirements Definition (Business)

A documented process is in place by which the project manager solicits and receives inputs and develops business requirements. The result is documentation for business requirements. There is a documented process in place by which the project manager seeks/receives management sign-offs (from either individual manager or management team) to approve the business requirements.

Requirements Definition (Technical)

Deliverables have some quantitative/qualitative basis behind them — that is, the deliverables should be performed in a specific way. There is a basic process for establishing a base set of deliverables for a project. The project manager (or team) always verifies project scope (what is to be included/excluded in project) with the client area. Management signs off on the technical aspects/expectations for the planned deliverables; there is agreement on how those deliverables will operate when produced.

Work Breakdown Structure

There is a basic process defined that includes a top-level WBS template (probably first and second levels) showing the organization's preferred primary project work breakdown structure). From the second WBS level on, the WBS is structured such that it has a built-in codification structure (task numbering) so that management reporting can "roll up" and take place rather naturally, consistent with the organizational requirements. There is a WBS template available that goes down to at least the third level (the level at which the structure begins to flesh out *how* each of the product groups defined in the first and second levels is to be delivered — the final level in this structure will define the tasks for the project). Management reviews and approves the WBS developed for new projects. Because of management's involvement, many of the projects in the organization that are medium-to-high levels of complexity have developed a comprehensive WBS for the project. These WBS structures are used to develop the project schedule, and as a communication vehicle with the sponsor, as the primary communication vehicle for the status of the project, etc.

Scope Change Control

There is a defined and documented scope change control process, but not all of the projects follow this process. Management supports the documented scope change control process and monitors to ensure it is being followed for larger, more visible projects. For those projects, there is a high degree of compliance in following the scope change control process.

Level 3
Organizational Standards and Institutionalized Process

There is a full, rigorous project management process documented and standardized for the organization; this process is in use by nearly all of the projects. All project management processes involve the clients as active and integral members of the project team. This team develops requirements, scope, and so on. The team as a unit seeks management input and approval of key decisions and documents; management is actively and integrally involved in key project decisions and issues. Stakeholder management is involved in the scope management process. The process requires, and management is actively participating in, key decisions where they pertain to project scope issues.

Scope Planning and Management

A Project Scope Management Plan template exists and is consistently used for all projects. This document defines, in considerable detail, how the project scope is to be defined and controlled.

Requirements Definition (Business)

There is a documented process in place that specifically prescribes the steps by which the project manager goes about the creation of the business requirements. This process involves all stakeholders: the business unit, the technical unit(s), other supporting organizations, and the client organization. This process may involve the utilization of facilitated rapid application development (RAD) techniques where all stakeholders come together to flesh out the business requirements, or a more traditional method whereby all stakeholders are involved in the analysis process. This process provides for the formation of the integrated project team, which is fully responsible for the requirements: creation, documentation, full understanding, agreement, and sign-off. The team sign-off is followed by management sign-offs at the business unit level, the technical level, and the client level.

Requirements Definition (Technical)

There is in place a standard format for technical specifications and a standard process by which these specifications are produced. This "standard process" may be a widely recognized process such as James Martin, LBMS, etc., but it is a detailed process (set of steps) through which the specifications for the deliverables are produced. This process is used on a continuing and ongoing basis. The integrated project team has key input into the technical requirements and specifications. This represents an additional step toward an integrated/facilitative process where the project team develops the requirements and specifications and thereby is buying into the process and its products.

Work Breakdown Structure

The WBS is always determined and documented by the fully integrated project team using a facilitated process that includes the business unit, technical groups, strategic groups as necessary, the client, etc. The WBS is always the basis for determining project tasks. Management is involved with development and approval of project WBS.

Scope Change Control

The scope change control system, reporting, and analysis processes are followed by the project teams (scope changes/status are being identified, evaluated, managed, and stakeholders are informed). A performance measurement process is developed and documented to evaluate project scope status and take corrective actions. The process is documented and repeatable. Baselines are established, adhered to, and managed.

Level 4
Managed Process

All project management processes are in place, being actively used on all projects, and are the normal (assumed) method of performing projects. There is an "organizational view" of all projects — even from within any single project. *Each project is evaluated and managed in light of other active projects.* Organizational management:

• Understands its role in the project management process

• Is regularly involved in the project management process

• Manages at "the right level" (delegating when appropriate and managing at a lower level when necessary)

• Holds the project managers and the project teams accountable for deployment against a comprehensive project management process on appropriate levels of projects (that is, on large, complex projects all steps of the project management process should be performed, all project management deliverables created, etc. — but on smaller, simpler projects a scaled-down set of steps and deliverables should be followed)

• Is managing against the improved process, not against the basic process.

Scope Planning and Management

Scope planning and management is actively used on all projects. The Project Scope Management Plan is used and accepted by the team. Scope planning and management is tailored to the size and type of project involved, as well as the organizational environment.

Requirements Definition (Business)

Business requirements are fully documented by the project team. The business requirements take careful account of other existing functions, systems, and other active projects. If, in the course of deploying the project, changes come about that affect the business requirements, the change control analysis should include an analysis of impacts on existing functions and other active projects.

Requirements Definition (Technical)

Technical requirements/specifications are fully documented by the project team, based in part on organizational standards. These specifications are created only after an analysis of ramifications of the proposed system on the current technical environment, other existing systems (interfaces, as well as performance ramifications), and other active projects.

Work Breakdown Structure

The WBS is included in the change control process. The creation of the WBS is closely aligned with documentation of deliverables. This process identifies that there are acceptable levels of change to the WBS that the project manager can make without approval. The project manager understands that WBS changes having impact on scope, time, or cost (or other major decisions) must be approved at the appropriate level of the organization.

Scope Change Control

All processes are in place, documented, and being utilized. The scope change control system is integrated with the organization's control systems, monitoring programs, and risk management process. Scope, cost, and schedule reports are integrated with technical status reports.

Level 5
Optimizing Process

The organization now has its focus not only on effectively managing all projects, but also on *improving the manner* in which future projects can be managed — that is, on process improvements. Projects are managed with *high utilization of value considerations.* Effectiveness and efficiency metrics are regularly calculated and tracked. There is a clear understanding of a project's value to the organization; all changes, issues, etc. are evaluated based upon effectiveness and efficiency metrics. Scope determinations are made/ decided at the appropriate level of management, based upon quantitative metrics determined by the project team.

Scope Planning and Management

Value and improvement are key considerations when planning scope definition and management. The Project Scope Management Plan includes instruction for measuring value of scope changes, considerations for cost of "rigor" applied to each project, and a process for recording and disseminating lessons learned.

Requirements Definition (Business)

There is full change control on business requirements. Any change is only initiated if it is fully understood and documented; management has approval at appropriate levels. Incorporates quality assurance techniques. Also incorporates quality improvement processes on an ongoing basis such that history is kept on how past projects defined and documented business requirements; this history is used to determine improvements in the process used for understanding and documenting business requirements. Change decisions for improvements, modifications, and additions to business requirements should include a judgment as to value: dollar impact, time impact, etc. There should be value metrics in place for making such decisions.

Requirements Definition (Technical)

There is full change control on requirements/ specifications. Any change is only initiated if it is fully understood and documented; management has approval at appropriate levels. Incorporates quality assurance techniques; incorporates quality improvement processes on an ongoing basis. All major projects are examined during the close process to ascertain needed changes to technical standards. There is a process in place whereby these changes are regularly incorporated. The decisions for any change in scope relative to technical requirements/ specifications must be based upon a value proposition: dollar impact, time impact, some value impact. There must be metrics involved in such decisions.

Work Breakdown Structure

The process of determining WBS and work plans is regularly examined (generally at project close-down) to ascertain lessons learned regarding process improvements. WBS and work plans are regularly monitored carefully and projected changes are foreseen and carefully documented. They are carefully evaluated based upon value propositions (cost/time/value) before the determination is made whether or not to proceed with the change.

Scope Change Control

An improvement process is in place to continuously improve the scope control process. Lessons learned are captured and used to improve the monitoring and control efforts. Metrics are gathered and analyzed to ascertain the accuracy of the scoping process. Scope variances are incorporated into the determination of project efficiency and effectiveness. A process utilizing scope variances and cost assessments for management decisions during project execution is developed, documented, and in place. Lessons learned are being captured.

CHAPTER 5

Project Time Management

THE OVERALL PURPOSE of time management is to develop the project schedule, manage to that schedule, and ensure the project completes within the approved time frame. Time management involves defining project activities, identifying required resources, sequencing the activities, developing the schedule, executing the schedule, and controlling the plans during project execution.

Components

Activity and Resource Definition

Activity definition involves identifying and documenting project activities that must be accomplished to produce the product(s) or services identified in the work breakdown structure. Resource definition and planning includes identifying what resources and quantities are needed for the project. Resources can include labor category, hours, material, and equipment. The outcome of this component is a list of all activities with any supporting detail including activity definitions, a listing of the project resource requirements, constraints, and assumptions.

Activity Sequencing

> Activity sequencing involves sequencing project activities and depicting when each product or service must be accomplished relative to other activities. Activity sequencing also includes the development of dependencies between activities. The outcome of this component is a project network diagram.

Schedule Development

> Schedule development involves determining the duration and calculating the start and finish dates for each project activity. Using the project network diagram, activity durations are established, resource requirements are confirmed, a project schedule is created, and a baseline schedule is established. This component includes the development of a schedule management plan. The main products from schedule development include the project schedule and a schedule management plan.

Schedule Control

> Schedule control involves managing the schedule baseline to ensure the project completes within the approved time frame. Managing the schedule baseline involves implementing a schedule control system, publishing schedule status reports, analyzing schedule performance metrics, determining changes to the schedule baseline, managing the authorized changes, informing stakeholders, and taking corrective action. The main products from this component include schedule reports, schedule performance analyses, and revised schedule baselines.

Schedule Integration

Schedule integration involves the integration of major components of project schedules. Schedules are integrated throughout the organization to accurately understand the impact of change. Program schedules reflect the integration of projects within a program to accurately understand the impact of project changes on the overall program. The main products of this component are integrated project, program, and organizational schedules.

Level 1
Initial Process

There is recognition of accepted processes, but there are no established practices or standards. Individual teams or parts of the organization may have their own way of doing things in an ad hoc, informal fashion. Documentation of the processes is loose and makes it difficult to repeat the activities elsewhere. Management is aware of the importance of time management and has periodically asked for schedule metrics.

Activity and Resource Definition

Generally, a scope statement is prepared for projects and the work breakdown structure consists of a basic set of milestones and occasionally deliverables. The project schedule is at the milestone level. Few or no activities are defined to achieve the milestones. Key milestones for functional support areas are sometimes overlooked. Project managers have developed their own way of identifying resources and quantities needed (labor category, hours, equipment, material). Functional support areas are sometimes overlooked. The way things are done is ad hoc, not documented, and varies by project (milestones are not standard).

Activity Sequencing

Project activities are sequenced on an ad hoc basis, if at all. If project activities are sequenced, they seldom reflect dependencies. Individual project teams may have access to and understand sequencing methods, but they are not standardized throughout the organization. Network diagrams with dependencies do not usually exist.

Schedule Development

There is no organizational process (only an ad hoc approach) for developing a schedule that includes using the network diagram, determining activity durations, identifying and prioritizing resources, developing the schedule, and baselining the project. Schedule development is ad hoc and is typically limited to independent milestones. Durations between milestones are rough guesses. Project managers have developed their own way of identifying resources and quantities needed. There is an ad hoc approach to finding who is available to work on projects. No help is available from the project office in developing the schedule or identifying a scheduling tool. Project teams and segments of the organization may have varying ways of developing a schedule baseline using milestones. There is no tool commonality in the organization.

Schedule Control

Individual project teams and segments of the organization are applying their own approach to managing and controlling schedules. Schedule milestone changes are unequally managed and, in many cases, not monitored, and changes seldom involve corrective actions. Ad hoc schedule reports are provided upon request. Schedule performance (metrics) is tracked using inconsistent and nonstandard practices.

Schedule Integration

Occasionally, there is an informal ad hoc grouping of project schedules for umbrella program schedules or integrated organization schedules. On request, individuals group together project schedules to depict program milestone status and organization-wide accomplishments.

Level 2
Structured Process and Standards

There are basic, documented processes in place for identifying project activities, sequencing the activities and establishing dependencies, developing summary schedules, publishing and distributing reports, and monitoring basic schedule metrics. Although the processes are in place, they are not considered an organizational standard. Basic metrics exist for schedule information (milestone percent complete) although they may be collected and correlated manually. Additional processes are developed and documented for activity definition, schedule development, and managing and controlling the schedule. A mix of summary and detailed information is developed and collected. Project management processes are considered standard practice for large, visible projects. All documented processes are repeatable. Management supports project management, but they are only consistently involved on large, visible projects.

Activity and Resource Definition

Generally, a scope statement is prepared and a scope process exists; however, management does not require adherence to the process. Summary activities are defined for near-term and long-term efforts. There is a basic, documented process for defining activities with standard milestones/exit criteria established for projects. Large, highly visible projects are using the basic process, WBS template, and standard milestones/exit criteria. Scope statements are prepared as standard practice on large, visible projects. There is a WBS template that goes down to at least level three. The project schedule is at a detailed level for large, visible projects. Detailed-level activities are defined to achieve the scope, at least level three in the WBS, milestones, and deliverables. Detailed activities and the resources required for these activities are defined for near-term efforts. The activity definition process is expanded to collect historical information (activities on similar projects). The activity definition process is documented and repeatable. The top-level WBS template, an identified set of key milestones/exit criteria, and the activity definition process are standardized for large, visible projects. Small projects are encouraged to use the process.

A complete resource listing is defined for all labor categories, equipment, and material. Everyone is encouraged to utilize the listing as a checklist for identifying resources (it is standard practice for large, highly visible projects). A planning process is developed and documented to include the resource listing and methodologies for determining quantities. The organization has industry standard tools, techniques, and/or factors for the project teams to approximate quantities but the use of these assists is not mandatory. The planning process is supported by management and is becoming accepted throughout the organization. The generic resource listing is incorporated into the project office's resource repository and project-specific requirements are manually inserted into the repository.

Activity Sequencing

The organization has a basic, documented process for sequencing activities and establishing precedence and dependencies. The activity sequence process includes the formal identification of constraints and assumptions that impact the sequencing of activities. The entire process for sequencing activities and establishing precedence and dependencies is a standard for large, visible projects. The organization has access to different activity sequencing methods (precedence, arrow, and conditional diagramming). Mandatory dependencies are identified at a summary level. Network diagrams exist at a summary level with mandatory dependencies. Both discretionary and mandatory dependencies are identified at the detailed level. Network diagrams exist at the detailed level with discretionary and mandatory dependencies.

Schedule Development

The basic guidelines represent a full, documented, repeatable process for developing schedules. In addition, the process includes the development of a historical database to collect data on activity durations. A schedule management plan and process is developed and documented. Large, highly visible projects use the processes as a standard, and other projects are encouraged to apply the processes. The project office closely monitors and supports the determination of project activity durations, development of schedules, and establishment of project baselines. It is the norm to have a project schedule at a detailed level (showing the level at which the structure begins to flesh out the deliverables for each product/service group). To calculate durations, project teams rely upon expert knowledge and access to industry methods, commercial databases, and industry standards and factors. Factors and standards may include capability and resource dedication measures. The organization has a complete resource listing, industry standard tools, techniques, and/or factors for project teams to approximate quantities. Teams develop staffing plans and work with line management to acquire resources. The resources are inserted into the schedule. Cost estimates are used to support schedule development. Project risks are considered. The organization has a documented process for allocating, timephasing, and baselining a project. Baselines are established, but may change frequently. Project management software tools are standard for large, visible projects and integration (dependency) is accomplished within projects. The organization has access to different scheduling methods: deterministic CPM (specified network logic and single duration estimates); probabilistic GERT (probabilities in network logic and duration estimates); and weighted average PERT (sequential network logic and weighted average duration estimates).

Schedule Control

A process is developed and documented for managing and controlling schedules and the concept of a schedule change control system is introduced. The process includes items such as schedule statusing, a change control form, a change log, and an issues log/form. Summary and detailed schedule reports are developed and provided to key stakeholders. The schedule reports are produced from a central system. Schedules are statused and tracked using planned versus actuals and milestone percent complete. Schedule baselines are established, but may change frequently. The organization is capable of simple variance analysis of schedule status (using planned status versus actual status). Metrics are collected such as schedule baseline, planned status, and actual status.

84 Schedule Integration

At the summary level, project schedules are manually grouped together to depict program schedules and organization-wide schedules. There is no attempt to integrate the dependencies and relationships within program schedules or the organization-wide schedules. At the summary and detailed levels, project schedules are still manually grouped together to depict program schedules and organization-wide schedules. Thought is being given to integrate program and organization-wide schedules. Guidelines to integrate schedules are in the early stages of formulation.

Level 3
Organizational Standards and Institutionalized Process

All processes are in place and documented. The processes are considered an organizational standard and are being utilized by nearly all of the projects. The activity definition process is expanded to include activity templates. Activity sequencing is expanded to include external dependencies and activity network templates. The schedule control process is expanded to include schedule performance analysis. The schedule integration process is developed and implemented with program schedules. Metrics are collected and analyzed in areas such as the number of project activities, type of external dependencies, duration standards, capability factors, resource dedication factors, and schedule performance and efficiency. Management fully supports the schedule management processes and has institutionalized the procedures and standards. Processes and standards are integrated with other corporate processes and systems. Integration includes organization-wide integration of projects with key dependencies established and monitored. In addition, the schedule development, schedule baselining, and cost control processes are integrated with the project office, finance/accounting, strategic planning systems, and risk management process. There is a mandate to comply with the organizational project management processes and procedures. Management takes an organizational view of projects.

Activity and Resource Definition

Scope statements with project assumptions and constraints are an organizational standard for all projects. The WBS is always used as the basis for determining project activities. This information is used to define activities and the required resources. A detailed schedule with detailed activities is the organizational standard practice. Detailed activities are defined for near-term efforts and beyond, if appropriate. Project teams are beginning to identify external, dependent activities. Historical information on common activities exists, and the activity definition process is expanded to include activity templates with definitions specific to the organization. The activity definition process is documented and repeatable. The activity templates are integrated into the standard scheduling software environment. Metrics are being collected such as the number of activities per project. Definition of project activities includes key tasks external to the project that may impact the project (external dependencies) and that need to be monitored and managed. The external activities may be program-related and/or organization-related.

With regard to resources, the planning process is fully implemented within the organization. Documentation exists on all planning processes and standards for identifying resource requirements. The project's resource requirements are uploaded into the project office's resource repository. Metrics are collected and analyzed on the types of resources required by projects and the resource availability to determine organizational efficiency in identifying and staffing resources. Use of industry standard tools, techniques and/or factors to approximate quantities is mandatory for all projects.

Activity Sequencing

The activity sequencing process is expanded to include external dependencies and activity network templates. The network templates depict common, sequenced activities with dependencies. The repeatable process is an organizational standard for all projects. Project teams document their network diagram approach, and unusual aspects are documented. Network diagrams exist at the detailed level with discretionary, mandatory, and external dependencies. The network templates are integrated into the standard scheduling software environment. Historical information is being collected such as the type of external dependencies.

Schedule Development

It is the norm to have a project schedule at appropriate levels of detail in line with the project scope and WBS. The historical database is established and the organization is starting to collect and analyze actual project durations for similar activities. To calculate durations, project teams may rely upon expert knowledge, industry standards, simulation techniques, and several organization-specific standards and factors. The resource process to identify resource requirements is fully implemented within the organization. The scheduling process is fully integrated with the project office, strategic planning systems, and risk management process. The project office centrally manages resource prioritization. Baselines are established, adhered to, and managed. Project management software tools are standard for all projects and projects are integrated within program areas. Cost and schedule information is integrated. Metrics are collected and analyzed in areas such as duration standards, capability factors, and resource dedication factors. All processes are in place, documented, and being utilized. Cost and schedule information is integrated with technical information.

Schedule Control

The schedule change control system, schedule reporting process, and earned value analysis processes are followed by project teams. Schedule changes/status are being identified, evaluated, managed, and stakeholders are informed. A performance measurement process is developed and documented to evaluate project schedule status and take corrective action. Schedule baselines are established, adhered to, and managed. Cost and schedule reports are integrated. Performance metrics (such as schedule variance and estimates at completion) are monitored and analyzed, and corrective actions are implemented. All processes are in place, documented, and being utilized. The schedule change control system is integrated with the organization's control systems, monitoring programs, and risk management process. Cost and schedule reports are integrated with technical reports.

Schedule Integration

A process is developed and documented to integrate program and organization-wide schedules. The process is used for program schedules to depict and integrate program schedules at summary and detailed levels. The program integration is centrally conducted, easily accomplished, and the process is repeatable. A process, system, and approach is employed for integrating programs and schedules across the organization. The organization develops, distributes, and analyzes integrated program schedules and integrated master schedules for the organization. Key external dependencies are identified, monitored, and managed. A program and organizational view is portrayed and analyzed.

Level 4
Managed Process

Projects are managed with consideration to how the project performed in the past and what is expected for the future. Management uses efficiency and effectiveness metrics to make decisions regarding the project. All projects, changes, and issues are evaluated based upon metrics from the schedule baselines, planned status, actual status, and schedule performance efficiency. The metrics are used to understand the performance of a project during execution for making management decisions for the future. Processes and standards are integrated with other corporate processes and systems. Integration includes the resource planning, scheduling, and budgeting process with the project office and human resources management process.

Activity and Resource Definition

All processes are in place, documented, and being utilized. Project activities are regularly monitored, focusing on information that is dependent upon other projects or programs throughout the organization. Management uses this information to make decisions regarding the project and related efforts. A process focusing on this information for making management decisions is developed, documented, and in place. Lessons learned are being captured. The planning process is fully integrated with the project office (for resource prioritization and scheduling) and the human resources project management process (for resource acquisition, assignment, and forecasts).

Activity Sequencing

Project dependencies are regularly monitored, focusing on dependencies between projects and programs throughout the organization. Management uses the dependent relationships to support decisions regarding the project and related efforts. A process utilizing project dependencies to understand the full impact of management decisions is developed, documented, and in place. Lessons learned are being captured.

Schedule Development

Baseline estimates (both revised and original) are not only used to manage individual projects, but are also used to make management decisions regarding project execution. Resource utilization is maximized and variance reports measure performance metrics of efficiency and effectiveness. Schedule status is used to support management decision-making. A process utilizing baseline, resource utilization measurements, and schedule status for management decisions is developed, documented, and in place. Lessons learned are being captured. The baseline process is fully integrated with the organization's strategic planning systems and risk management process.

Schedule Control

Schedule assessments are incorporated and included in the determination of project efficiency and effectiveness. For certain projects, earned value and performance status reporting is integrated with cost and schedule systems. The schedule supports earned value analysis and the capability exists to calculate the budgeted cost of work scheduled and performed, and schedule estimate at completion. All earned value techniques are used, including performance indices, to compare project performance to the project baseline and make forecasts, as appropriate. Earned value techniques are used to update project schedules (revise the baseline costs) and to support the determination of project efficiency and effectiveness. A process using schedule assessments and earned value techniques for management decisions during project execution is developed, documented, and in place. Lessons learned are being captured.

Schedule Integration

Management makes decisions understanding the full impact across programs and the organization. A process utilizing the integrated program and organization schedules for management decisions during project execution is developed, documented, and in place. Lessons learned are being captured. Independent audits have been introduced to identify and recommend areas for improvement.

Level 5
Optimizing Process

Improvement procedures are in place and utilized. Lessons learned are regularly examined and used to improve documented processes. Past performance is utilized as a tool to improve future performance.

Activity and Resource Definition

A process is in place to continuously improve activity definition to completely identify all activities effectively and efficiently using templates, past experience, and industry standards. The process improvement will also focus on ensuring all constraints and assumptions are properly identified and captured.

An improvement process is also in place to continuously improve resource planning to completely identify all resource requirements as early as possible, and in the right quantities. Lessons learned are captured and used to improve resource-planning efforts. The planning process includes a method to identify an organizational priority for obtaining additional resources during project execution. The priority designator is linked to the management decisions and gives project teams the ability to identify the priority of their resource requests. The enhanced process is developed, documented, and in place.

Activity Sequencing

An improvement process is in place to continuously improve activity sequencing to better identify mandatory, discretionary, and external dependencies and to determine when each product or service must be accomplished relative to other activities. Lessons learned are captured and used to improve activity-sequencing efforts.

Schedule Development

An improvement process is in place to continuously improve the schedule definition process of using the project network diagram, establishing activity durations, confirming resource requirements, creating a project schedule, and establishing a baseline. The improvement process will also focus on the schedule management plan. Lessons learned are captured and used to improve the schedule-definition effort.

Schedule Control

An improvement process is in place to continuously improve the schedule control process, including schedule-performance analyses. Lessons learned are captured and used to improve the monitoring and control efforts.

Schedule Integration

A process is in place to continuously improve the schedule integration process for programs and across the organization. Lessons learned are captured and used to improve the measuring effort.

CHAPTER 6

Project Cost Management

THE OVERALL PURPOSE of cost management is to determine the total costs of the project, manage to those costs, and ensure the project completes within the approved budget. Cost management involves estimating the cost of identified resources, developing a project baseline, comparing progress against the baseline, and controlling costs.

Components

Cost Estimating

Cost estimating is an analytical process using factors, equations, relationships, and expert knowledge to develop the cost of a product, service, or process. If detailed resources are identified, cost estimating applies rates and factors to determine the cost. The main outcome is a project cost estimate and a cost management plan.

Cost Budgeting

Cost budgeting involves developing a project cost baseline by allocating the cost estimate to individual elements in the work breakdown structure. Cost budgeting includes timephasing the cost estimate to develop the baseline. The main product of this component is a project cost baseline.

Performance Measurement

Earned value involves measuring the project performance to determine whether work has been accomplished in accordance with plans. Earned value uses the cost baseline and compares actual performance against the baseline plan. The main products are a comparison of actuals to the baseline and earned value metrics.

Cost Control

Cost control involves managing the cost baseline to ensure the project completes within the approved budget. Managing the cost baseline involves implementing a cost control system, publishing cost status reports, analyzing cost performance metrics, determining changes to the cost baseline, managing the authorized changes, informing stakeholders, and taking corrective action. The main products from this component include cost reports, cost performance analyses, revised project cost baseline, and lessons learned.

Level 1
Initial Process

There is recognition of accepted processes, but there are no established practices or standards. Individual teams or parts of the organization may have their own way of doing things in an ad hoc, informal fashion. Documentation of the processes is loose and makes it difficult to repeat the activities elsewhere. Management is aware of the importance of cost management and has periodically asked for cost metrics.

Cost Estimating

Estimates are developed on an ad hoc basis and may or may not capture all costs. Generally, the project manager will have a scope statement and a schedule that consists of a basic set of milestones, and occasionally deliverables, to determine what to estimate. The documentation for the estimates is incomplete, limited, and not required by the organization. Individual project teams may have access to some tools and techniques, but they are not standardized throughout the organization.

Cost Budgeting

Project teams and segments of the organization may have adopted ways of developing a cost baseline (allocating and timephasing the cost estimate). There is no established practice, and documentation of the processes is incomplete.

Performance Measurement

Project performance analysis is calculated on an ad hoc basis and done informally. Periodically simple performance metrics are developed (e.g., planned budget and major milestones). There is no established practice or procedure; individuals follow their own methods. The validity and consistency of the information is suspect since standards are not in place.

Cost Control

Individual project teams and segments of the organization are applying their own approach to managing and controlling costs. Cost changes are unequally managed and, in many cases, not monitored. Ad hoc cost reports are provided on a by-request basis. When cost performance is tracked, it is by the use of nonstandard practices.

Level 2
Structured Process and Standards

There are documented processes in place for identifying generic key resources (labor categories, hours, equipment, and material), generating and documenting project cost estimates, publishing and distributing reports, and monitoring basic cost metrics. Although the processes are in place, they are not considered an organizational standard. Management supports the efforts and is involved on large, highly visible projects. A basic cost-estimating template exists. Metrics exist for basic cost information (planned budget, percent complete) although they may be collected and correlated manually. Additional processes are likely to exist for resource cost planning, historical cost database development, earned value techniques, cost reporting, and cost performance analysis. Summary and detailed information is developed and collected. Project management processes are considered standard practice for large, visible projects. All documented processes are repeatable.

Cost Estimating

The organization has a documented process for generating and documenting project cost estimates. Generally, a scope statement is prepared, a top-level WBS template (levels one and two showing the organization's preferred primary project work breakdown structure) exists, and a summary schedule is normally in place. These items support the development of summary-level estimates for the upper levels of the WBS. A basic cost-estimating template is established (may include things such as description of item, WBS element, work hours estimate, number of resources, equipment, material, travel, risk factors, source of estimate, and key assumptions). Average resource billing rates are developed for generic resources. A cost-estimating historical database exists to develop cost standards and factors. A cost management plan and process is developed, documented, and is standard practice on large, visible projects. The organization has access to tools, techniques, commercial databases, and industry cost standards and factors, and organization-specific cost standards and factors are in the early formulation stages. Scope statements are prepared as standard practice on large, visible projects. It is the norm to have a project schedule at least to level three in the WBS. The capability exists to estimate most levels of the WBS (using the scope statement and WBS template) resulting in detailed project cost estimates, as appropriate. Project risks are considered. A system is in place to record project estimates and collect actuals ("estimated" actuals from project teams versus accounting actuals from corporate systems) for future comparison. Average resource rates are developed for resources where standards can be established.

Cost Budgeting

Baselining is not yet common practice nor established as an organizational standard, except for large, highly visible projects. The organization has a documented process for allocating, timephasing, and baselining a project. The project has a staff management plan that supports the development of the time-phased baseline. The capability exists to baseline projects, and most projects are developing and documenting project baselines at differing levels of detail. Baselines are established in line with the project schedule, but may change frequently.

Performance Measurement

The organization is capable of tracking summary-level hours and budget and tracking progress toward achieving milestones. The basic process is documented. Basic metrics such as planned budget and milestone percent complete are utilized. The organization is capable of simple variance analysis of project hours (using planned versus actuals). Metrics such as planned budget, planned hours, hours spent, and delta are established. A system is in place to collect "estimated" project actuals (normally hours) from the project teams (versus extracting accounting information from corporate systems).

Cost Control

A process is developed and documented to publish and distribute cost reports. Periodic cost reports are developed at the summary level and provided to key stakeholders. Summary cost reports are produced from an integrated system. Basic cost metrics (planned budget and percent complete) are collected and reported. A process is developed and documented for managing and controlling cost and the concept of a cost change control system is introduced. The process includes items such as cost statusing, a change control form, a change log, and an issues log/form. Baselines are established in line with the project schedule, but may change frequently. Summary and detailed cost reports are developed and provided to key stakeholders. "Estimated" project actuals are provided by the project teams (versus extracting accounting actuals from corporate systems).

Level 3
Organizational Standards and Institutionalized Process

All processes are in place and documented. The processes are considered an organizational standard and are being utilized by nearly all projects. The cost-estimating process is expanded to include analyses of alternatives. The performance measurement process is expanded beyond simple variance analyses. The cost change control system is in place and implemented. All processes are repeatable. Systems are becoming more integrated: resource requirements are uploaded into the project office's resource repository, project baselining is integrated with the project office's automated scheduling system (or something comparable), and cost reporting is easily accomplished. Metrics are collected and analyzed on the types of resources, cost estimates, and project performance and efficiency. The project teams reconcile "estimated" actuals versus accounting actuals from corporate financial/accounting systems. Management fully supports the cost management processes and has institutionalized the procedures and standards.

Cost Estimating

The cost-estimating process is further expanded to include cost analyses of alternatives. The entire process is fully documented and repeatable. The process outlined within the cost management plan is in place and implemented. Several organization-specific cost standards and factors are developed. Comparisons are made between actual project costs (forecasts based upon actuals-to-date) and the original estimates. Metrics are collected, analyzed, and reported. The historical database is established, and data are collected and analyzed for future reference and quantitative application.

Cost Budgeting

Projects are developing and documenting project baselines at the lowest reasonable level. The baselines are established in line with the project schedule. The capability exists to enter the time-phased estimates into the project software environment (or something comparable) at any appropriate level of detail. The baseline process is fully integrated with the project office's project schedule system (or something comparable), documented, and repeatable. Baselines are established, adhered to, and managed.

Performance Measurement

The performance measurement process is expanded beyond basic variance calculations to include earned value analysis on appropriate projects. The full process is documented and repeatable. The capability exists to calculate the budgeted cost of work scheduled and performed, the actual cost of work performed, budget at completion, and estimate at completion. Metrics include basic performance measurement calculations with actuals provided by the project teams versus corporate financial/ accounting systems.

Cost Control

The cost change control process, cost-reporting process, and performance measurement analysis processes are followed and utilized by the project teams (cost changes/status are being identified, evaluated, managed, and stakeholders are informed). Baselines are established, adhered to, and managed. Cost and schedule reports are integrated. Earned value and performance status reporting is integrated with cost and schedule systems. Performance metrics (such as schedule variance, cost variance, and estimates at completion) are monitored, analyzed, and corrective actions are implemented. The project teams reconcile "estimated" actuals versus accounting actuals from corporate financial/accounting systems.

Level 4
Managed Process

Processes and standards are integrated with other corporate processes and systems. Integration includes the resource planning process with the project office and human resources management process. In addition, the cost-estimating, cost-baselining, earned value, and cost control processes are integrated with the project office, finance/accounting, strategic planning systems, and risk management process. Actuals are provided by the corporate financial/accounting systems and analyzed by the project teams. There is a mandate to comply with the organizational project management processes and procedures. Management takes an "organizational view" of projects.

Cost Estimating

All processes are in place, documented, and being utilized. The cost-estimating process is fully integrated with the project office, finance/accounting, strategic planning systems, and risk management process. Organization-specific cost standards and factors exist for elements of the WBS that are consistently used and standard in projects.

Cost Budgeting

All processes are in place, documented, and being utilized. The baselining process is fully integrated with the scheduling, the organization's finance/accounting, strategic planning systems, and risk management process.

Performance Measurement

All earned-value techniques are used as appropriate on key projects where logical application provides measurable benefit, including performance indices, to compare project performance to the project baseline and make forecasts, as appropriate. Projects are employing such techniques, if applicable. The earned-value process is integrated with the organization's finance/accounting, strategic planning systems, and risk management process. Earned value is used to update project costs and revise the baseline costs, if applicable. Actuals are provided by the corporate financial/accounting systems and analyzed by the project teams.

Cost Control

All processes are in place, documented, and being utilized. The cost change control system is integrated with the organization's control systems, monitoring programs, and risk management process. Cost and schedule reports are integrated with technical status reports. Actuals are provided by the corporate financial/accounting systems and analyzed by the project teams. A performance measurement process is developed and documented to evaluate project cost status and take corrective action. The process is documented and repeatable.

<u>Level 5</u>
Optimizing Process

Improvement procedures are in place and utilized. Lessons learned are regularly examined and used to improve documented processes. Projects are managed with consideration as to how the project performed in the past and what is expected for the future. Management uses efficiency and effectiveness metrics to make decisions regarding the project. All projects, changes, and issues are evaluated based upon metrics from cost estimates, baseline estimates, and earned value. The metrics are used to understand the performance of a project during execution for making management decisions for the future.

Cost Estimating

An improvement process is in place to continuously improve cost estimating to better forecast project costs and improve the cost management plan. Lessons learned are captured and used to improve cost management efforts. Comparisons are made between forecasted project costs (based upon actuals-to-date) and the original estimates. Management uses this information to understand required resources for continued support to project activities and to make decisions regarding the project. A process utilizing cost estimates for making management decisions before and during project execution is developed, documented, and in place. Lessons learned are being captured.

Cost Budgeting

An improvement process is in place to continuously improve the cost-budgeting and baselining process. Lessons learned are captured and used to improve the baselining effort. Baseline estimates (both revised and original) are not only used to manage individual projects but are also used to make management decisions regarding project execution. A process utilizing baseline measurements for making management decisions during project execution is developed, documented, and in place. Lessons learned are being captured.

Performance Measurement

An improvement process is in place to continuously improve the earned value process. Lessons learned are captured and used to improve the measuring effort. Full earned-value techniques are used to update project costs (revise the baseline costs) and to support the determination of project efficiency and effectiveness. A process utilizing earned-value techniques for management decisions during project execution is developed, documented, and in place. Lessons learned are being captured.

Cost Control

An improvement process is in place to continuously improve the cost control process. Lessons learned are captured and used to improve the monitoring and control efforts. Cost assessments are incorporated and included in the determination of project efficiency and effectiveness. A process utilizing cost assessments for management decisions during project execution is developed, documented, and in place. Lessons learned are being captured.

CHAPTER 7

Project Quality Management

THE OVERALL PURPOSE of quality management is to satisfy the customer, to conform to requirements, to ensure fitness for purpose, and to ensure the product is fit for use. It is that set of activities/tasks that are required to ensure the project satisfies all the needs for which it was undertaken (and which are documented in the statement of work), and includes a focus on quality management from the perspective of product, processes, and the people needed to make quality an effective and efficient aspect of successful project completion.

Components

Quality Planning

Quality planning involves identifying quality standards, practices, and associated quality activities. Planning for quality should be done in parallel with other project planning processes. The main product from quality planning is the quality management plan, which identifies the specific quality practices, resources, and activities relevant to the project and its deliverables. It includes strategies for implementing quality assurance and control.

Quality Assurance

Quality assurance involves developing and assessing processes, procedures, and standards to assure the project will meet relevant quality standards.

Quality Control

Quality control involves monitoring actual project results to see if they comply with relevant quality standards and identifying ways to eliminate causes of unsatisfactory results. Quality control activities are the procedures necessary to ensure the project deliverables meet the quality objectives and attributes defined in the team's quality management plan.

Special Interest Component — Management Oversight

The overall purpose of management oversight is to understand, support, and be involved in project management activities. This includes the following two items:

Awareness and Support
Awareness and support involves management understanding and being cognizant of project management activities and advocating organization-wide implementation of project management processes and standards.

Involvement
Involvement covers management participation and inclusion in project management activities, processes, and standards.

Level 1
Initial Process

Management has an awareness of the need for quality management, but there are no established practices or standards. Management is considering how they should define "quality."

Quality Planning

Some project teams may develop high-level quality plans, but on an ad hoc basis, with each project manager doing as s/he sees fit.

Quality Assurance

There are no established practices or standards for quality assurance, but some project teams establish project procedures for their project teams and on an ad hoc basis check to make sure everyone is following the procedures.

Quality Control

There are no established practices or standards for quality control, but many project team members will have someone "look over" their work product before they submit it to management. On an ad hoc basis there may be testing applied to specific units or portions of the product for development-based projects (e.g., in an IT environment each analyst/ programmer does his/her own testing to see if his/ her part of the product works).

Management Oversight

Management recognizes that there are project management processes occurring within the organization on an ad hoc basis by individual project managers. Management understands the definition of a project and is aware of the need for project management.

Awareness and Support
Management is aware of project management processes and recognizes that there is a difference between the requirements for project management and operational management. Management supports individual interest in applying project management standards or processes on an ad hoc basis at the discretion of the project manager, but does not require any conformity of use.

Involvement
Management's involvement in daily project activities is limited to inquiring about project status, should the need arise for such information.

Level 2
Structured Process and Standards

A basic organizational quality policy has been adopted and management encourages the use of it on large and highly visible projects. Management is supportive of the time required to add quality to a project, such as defining and implementing quality control metrics into a project. The organization's quality policy has been bolstered to state the organization's quality objectives, the level of quality acceptable to the organization, and the roles/responsibilities of members of the organization for executing the policy and ensuring quality. Management takes an active role in ensuring that quality standards are accounted for and applied to most projects.

Quality Planning

The quality planning process has been enhanced to include such quality assurance processes as flowcharting and operational definitions (metrics) and quality control measures. Metrics include results of reviews and tests against criteria, specifications, quality standards, and business requirements. Most people in the organization consider the quality planning process as the standard way of ensuring quality is accounted for within the project products/services. Most of the projects — and all the large, highly visible projects — are actually using these quality planning processes, including the development of a quality management plan. Management signs off on the quality plans on these larger projects.

Quality Assurance

There is a basic approach for quality assurance. For large, highly visible projects, teams establish project procedures and use walkthroughs or peer reviews to assure the team is following procedures. The team may identify the points in the development process at which there may be a need for extra quality precautions. Quality assurance processes, including tools and techniques such as flowcharting and operational definitions, are considered standard approaches on large, highly visible projects. The project office provides a quality policy and project management processes and standards to support the quality assurance measures on projects. Project teams also have devised checklists for use in checking/ promoting quality throughout the project life cycle. Other project teams use tools and techniques, such as design of experiment concepts throughout the project.

Quality Control

The basic quality process includes suggested approaches for quality control, in that it provides guidelines for document review, hardware inspection and test, drawing checks, and testing specific units or portions of the product, first-level integration test (for development projects), and a review of individual project deliverables/products by the project team (e.g., in an IT environment guidelines are laid out for the testing of modules and programs, to ascertain that each part of the system works, and also for testing the system resulting when these modules and programs are integrated together). Summary-level testing metrics are collected and evaluated. The tools utilized include acceptance criteria, performance standards, business requirements, specifications, and quality standards for the reviews/testing. The quality control processes are used on large and highly visible projects and encouraged on all other projects. Full acceptance criteria and specifications are developed, including business requirements and quality standards. The quality process includes a document review process and templates and guidelines for:

- Deliverable and product testing (including evaluation by the customer)
- Unit testing (testing of the individual components of the product)
- Integration testing (testing how the major assemblies of the product work together).

The project team does unit and integration testing. Both summary-level and detailed testing metrics are collected and evaluated.

Management Oversight

Basic project management processes exist in the organization, but they are not considered an organizational standard — only large or highly visible projects are required to use them. Basic summary-level metrics have been established for projects to track project cost, schedule, and technical performance (triple constraint). Most project management processes are in place and are considered standard practice for larger, more visible projects. Management understands the value of project management and endorses its use throughout the organization. Although management is not consistently involved in the project management processes throughout the organization, they do take an active role and are consistently involved in the larger, more visible projects.

Awareness and Support

Management oversight on large or highly visible projects encourages the establishment of project cost, schedule, and technical performance planning and tracking and will provide the project managers with the tools or training required to develop such project planning elements. Management receives status reports and formal acceptance notification of project completion. Management supports the use of the standardized project management processes across the organization for all projects and will provide the training or tools required by project managers to implement these processes. Large or highly visible projects are required to implement these processes, as management recognizes that such processes are a contributing factor to project success.

Involvement

On large or highly visible projects, management encourages summary progress reporting of project performance at the milestone level for schedule and cost. If there are issues or changes that require management approval, management provides such on a requested basis. Management approves the project charter and assigns project managers. On large or highly visible projects, management plays an active role in requiring regular project status reports that show baselined project plans and the collection of actual performance metrics. On these projects, management expects to be apprised of project performance (and provides appropriate response), to be in the approval chain for change control items that impact the triple constraints, and to be in the issues management process for escalation and resolution of issues that cannot be resolved within the confines of

the project team. If requested, management will take
a more prominent role in small and medium-sized
projects, but otherwise only requires performance
reporting from project managers when called upon.
Management signs off on project completion.

Level 3
Organizational Standards and Institutionalized Process

The quality process is now well documented and is an organizational standard; most of the projects follow this standard. Management signs off on the quality plan and final testing for all projects and often participates in quality reviews. Quality has a program focus — that is, how well does the product perform within the context of all other products/systems in the immediate domain of the product? Management supports the development of a quality department and has identified one or two people whose focus is organizational project quality standards and assurance.

Quality Planning

The quality planning process has been enhanced to include guidelines for design of experiments (analytical techniques that help identify which variables have the most influence on the overall outcome), emphasis on quality milestones, and has standardized checklists for the use of the project teams in creating their quality plans. The process prescribes a formal quality plan and has templates for the creation of such; it includes organizational management at key approval points. The quality planning process now includes the scope/perspective of other entities in the immediate domain of the products of the project (e.g., in an IT environment, when a new system is the product, the systems with which this system interfaces are included in the quality plan). The organization has identified one or two people whose focus is organizational project quality standards and assurance.

Quality Assurance

Tools and techniques, such as design of experiments and quality assurance checklists, are now considered standard approaches on large, highly visible projects and are suggested approaches on all projects. Projects take on a proactive stance in quality and plans for regular walkthroughs with organizational management and other project teams as major portions of the product are developed to assure that the product will function correctly with other elements of the environment.

Quality Control

Project performance standards are identified and begin to be established and measured against. The quality process includes templates and guidelines for:

- Model office that emulates a production environment and allows for product testing in a simulated situation

- Interface testing (testing how the product works in its environment with other systems/products)

- Acceptance testing (testing the human interface and testing against the original requirements)

- Review of documents, drawings and inspection of hardware, to include re-work procedures.

The client is actively involved in product review and interface testing, although the actual testing is performed by the project team. The client *drives* acceptance testing — in fact, acceptance testing requires a signoff from both the client and management before being accepted as completed. The end-user, or client, is also the final acceptance station for any document, drawing, or hardware that is a contractual deliverable.

Management Oversight

All project management processes are in place, are repeatable, and most projects are expected to use them. These processes involve the clients as active and integral members of the project team. Management fully supports and has institutionalized the processes and standards. Management is regularly involved in input and approval of key decisions and documents and in key project issues.

Awareness and Support

Management is required to attend project management awareness training that is geared toward their role in project management and establishing expectations for project outcomes. Management supports the projects within the organization by ensuring they have visibility and prioritization. In addition, management recognizes and supports the discipline of project management as a profession unto itself, including the distinct roles within the field beyond project manager, such as project support-type roles and project leadership-type roles.

Involvement

Informal variance analysis, to compare project baseline and project actuals, is expected by management on most projects. This information is then used by management in evaluating the relative progress of the project compared to other projects. Management is actively involved in key critical decisions within the projects, including change control, issue escalation, risk response, quality assurance, and customer interaction. Management co-assigns project managers.

Level 4
Managed Process

Organizational management has mandated that all projects follow the quality planning standard processes. Nearly all of the projects employ them. Quality is viewed from an organizational perspective — the quality of the product is evaluated in light of all other products/systems in the environment and how well it will meet the business objectives. There is an established quality office within the organization responsible for quality standards and assurance to quality processes for all projects.

Quality Planning

The quality planning process now includes the perspective of the entire environment into which the product of the project is being placed. A quality office is established within the organization. The organization benchmarks its project results against industry standard results.

Quality Assurance

Projects regularly include walkthroughs with organizational management and other project teams as major portions of the product are developed to assure that the product will meet the business requirements and specifications. Documentation procedures are in place that require each major component (subsystem, database, interface, etc.) of the product to be fully documented prior to moving into a final production mode. Nearly all of the projects use quality assurance processes/methods as specified by the quality standards. Metrics collected throughout the project life cycle are regularly compared to industry standards to ascertain potential problem areas.

Quality Control

The organization has performance standards in place; project products are consistently reviewed, inspected and tested against these standards. The organization has functional standards in place; project products are consistently reviewed, checked and tested against these standards. The quality process includes templates and guidelines for review and testing that the products integrate with other products/systems in the organization, and that all portions of the organization affected in any way by the product have an opportunity to adequately test those effects.

Management Oversight

Project management processes are integrated with corporate processes. Management clearly understands its role in the project management process and executes it well, managing at the right level, and clearly differentiating management styles and project management requirements for different sizes/complexities of projects. An organizational mandate is in place to comply with the project management processes.

Awareness and Support
Management actively endorses the project management processes as key to organizational success by ensuring project outcomes are successful. For example, the project office has become integrated into the organizational framework as a full functioning area or division, management perceives value of projectizing the organization and the utilization of matrixed resources, and there is

resource pool management and efficiency and effectiveness performance measurements. Management also encourages the evolution of the project management profession within the organization and actively supports the need for both project management expertise and technical expertise on all projects.

Involvement
Formal variance analysis, to compare project baseline and project actuals, is expected by management on all projects. Management takes an active role in performance measurement metrics of efficiency and effectiveness on corporate systems and project management processes. Management regularly serves in project-related roles, such as project sponsor, executive change control board, customer liaison, and project mentoring.

Level 5
Optimizing Process

The quality process includes techniques/methods/guidelines for feeding improvements back into the process. The quality process focuses on the use of metrics in making benefit/cost comparisons, effectiveness and efficiency decisions, and final decision on the quality of the product.

Quality Planning

The quality planning process includes a process whereby the process itself is critiqued throughout the project. Lessons learned are actively utilized to improve the process for future projects. The quality planning process integrates the usage of metrics and data from earlier projects, and from earlier stages of the given project, to make benefit/cost comparisons and decisions regarding quality planning. The quality planning process uses the metrics and data collected to make value-related trade-off decisions regarding quality planning.

Quality Assurance

Feedback is gained from the quality assurance processes and is actively used to improve project management processes for future projects. Effectiveness and efficiency of both the product and the project processes are regularly measured using metrics collected throughout the project.

Quality Control

Quality control/testing results are examined on a regular basis throughout the project to ascertain improvements, which are integrated back into the process. Management uses quality control results to make decisions on the usability and fit of the product and when/if the product is acceptable. Quality Control results also directly effect the actual inspection, review and testing processes used to validate and verify deliverables.

Management Oversight

Improvement procedures are in place and utilized. Lessons learned are regularly examined and used to improve documented processes. Projects are given high value within the organization; thus there is high visibility to the individuals who are actively involved in projects on a regular basis. All projects, changes, and issues are evaluated based upon efficiency and effectiveness metrics, and management takes an active role in management oversight and executive sponsorship of projects within the organization. Projects are directly tied to the success of the organization; thus there is a financial tie to success of the organization and the project-related positions that are responsible for successful project performance.

Awareness and Support

An improvement process is in place to continuously improve management's awareness and support of corporate projects and their needs. Lessons learned are captured and used to improve the monitoring and control efforts. Projects are managed with consideration as to how the project performed in the past and what is expected for the future. Management is aware of the need to capture lessons learned and the value of making decisions based upon efficiency and effectiveness metrics.

Involvement

An improvement process is in place to continuously improve management's involvement in the process of managing projects. Lessons learned are captured and used to improve the monitoring and control efforts. Management uses the data obtained from the efficiency and effectiveness metrics for projects to make decisions. Lessons learned about management's involvement in project operations as related to overall project success are captured.

CHAPTER 8

Project Human Resource Management

THE OVERALL PURPOSE of human resource management is to identify the requisite skill sets required for specific project activities, to identify individuals who have those skill sets, and to assign roles and responsibilities for the project, managing and ensuring high productivity of those resources, and forecasting future resource needs.

Components

Human Resource Planning

This refers to the activities of identifying, documenting, and assigning project roles, responsibilities, and reporting relationships for the project.

Staff Acquisition

This covers identifying, soliciting, and acquiring the necessary resources for the project.

Develop and Manage Project Team

Team development is the act of creating synergy between project team members to enhance productivity, efficiency, and overall project success.

Are there guidelines and standards in place to promote team buy-in to the project? They should feel a part of the process of requirements analysis, scope development, etc. The project management team also tracks team member performance, provides feedback, and resolves issues.

Special Interest Component — Professional Development

The overall purpose of professional project management development is to develop the level of professionalism that exists within the organization's project manager and project team member resource pool, as well as to develop how the organization supports and views the professional requirements for project management. This is viewed by the following subcomponents:

Individual Project Management Knowledge
Individual knowledge base refers to the knowledge acquired by the individual in project management — a degree, a certificate, an awareness of the need for project management education.

Individual Project Management Experience/ Competence
This refers to the individual's actual experience in working on or leading projects. Examples of project experience include working as a project controller, planner/scheduler, estimator, project management process expert, methodologist, project administrative support (change control, action item, contract compliance, reporting, etc.) or mentor. Competency is measured by determining the effectiveness of an individual's work efforts, or an individual's ability to

successfully lead the delivery of projects of varying size and complexity.

Corporate Initiative for Project Management Development

If the corporation acknowledges project management as a cornerstone for building corporate success, then they will incorporate environmental success factors, such as formalized professional developmental programs or project management career path (including training, compensation, motivation, etc.) for their project managers and project team members.

Level 1
Initial Process

There is recognition within the organization of the need for a human resource project management process consisting of identifying resource requirements and "reserving" them; however, there are no established practices or standards. This ad hoc process is used to determine how many people would be required to accomplish project activities and define who is available. In general, the "warm-body" concept applies, which means that there is an assumption that any person can serve in whatever capacity necessary. Documentation is loose and may exist in the form of a list of people working on a project. As such, informal project teams may exist in an ad hoc sense. Metric data exist only from the standpoint of who worked on the last project, but are not required.

Human Resource Planning

There is an ad hoc process of determining how many people are required to work on project activities. An informal reporting relationship exists, such that project staff members know that they need to get their project assignments from the project manager.

Staff Acquisition

There is an ad hoc process of finding who is available to work on project activities and going to line management to ask to have certain resources for a project.

Develop and Manage Project Team

There is an ad hoc process of trying to ensure that project team members work together in a professional manner, which may include occasionally trying to get complementary personalities on the same project team. Occasional team meetings may be held whereby the team may be included in an explanation of the direction of the organization to the level that deliverables, scope, WBS, and the like have been defined.

Professional Development

There are pockets within the organization that have recognized that the skills and abilities required to successfully lead a project are different than for other job functions, and thus could be considered a separate job function. However, there are no corporate standards or processes in place from which one can build the justification for a professional project management career path. Individual managers may recognize and give credit to specific individuals for their project-related accomplishments, but this is done on an ad hoc and individual basis.

Individual Project Management Knowledge

Some individuals within the organization may be recognized or acknowledged for knowing more than others about some project management aspects, such as an ability to use a scheduling tool, an awareness of a budgeting mechanism, or an ability to develop a general project scope statement.

Individual Project Management Experience/ Competence

Some individuals within the organization may be recognized or acknowledged for successfully working on or managing a project. This success is considered unique to the abilities of the individual.

Corporate Initiative for Project Management Development

Some managers within the organization may have acknowledged or recognized the accomplishments of an individual who has worked on or has led a project with a successful outcome.

Level 2
Structured Process and Standards

There is a documented, repeatable process in place that defines how to define, acquire, and manage the human resources in the form of suggested inputs, tools and techniques, and outcomes. Formal teams are established on large projects that are held accountable to follow the human resource management process. Management expects the project manager to have a project management human resource plan (Staffing Management Plan) in place for large projects. Project team evaluations are conducted and project managers are expected to provide line management with a performance report for the individuals at the end of the project. Processes are readily available and integrated with other project planning elements.

Human Resource Planning

The project manager creates a basic overview of the types of skill sets that are required by the project and the approximate timeframe in which these skill sets are needed. Basic responsibility definition exists in the form of a responsibility assignment matrix by major deliverable. A project organization chart exists so that the individuals on the project know who reports to whom on the project. An informal analysis (which consists of the project team discussing these elements and defining their response, but no formal evaluation document produced for management) is conducted to define the organizational, technical, and interpersonal interfaces that exist within the organization. There is an understanding of the constraints that may be prevalent in attaining required resources, such as the type of organization (hierarchical to projectized), and individual preferences to work on one project or another. In addition to a project organization chart, there is a narrative description of the responsibilities for the key project personnel and a staffing plan that defines when resources will be needed. As the project progresses, measurement of planning versus actual will occur with regard to the staffing plan. Updated planning information will come from project integration and the staffing plan will provide corrective action, as necessary.

Staff Acquisition

Staff acquisition consists of identifying the individuals who have the requisite skill sets and time availability to work on the project. The project manager requests line management to reserve team members for a certain timeframe. A staffing requirements document will be submitted from cost management as an input for defining the staffing management plan. There is a "first come, first served" process in place whereby whoever requests a resource first gets usage of that resource first. In addition, when a resource is assigned by line management to a project, line management documents that resource's labor category, so that the project manager can utilize that information for costing purposes. If there is another project or assignment of extremely high priority, a resource may be withdrawn from a project by organizational management for a short period of time. The staffing management plan includes defining the parameters for the desired project team, including minimal experience, personal interests and characteristics, and availability to determine a good fit among project team members. However, the project manager must accept whatever resources are assigned by the line manager to the project. Project human resource management and the project office coordinate efforts in resource pool management.

Develop and Manage Project Team

Project teams may or may not have had an opportunity to work together before; as such, the projects are begun with an informal kickoff in which the team members are briefed on the purpose of the project, their responsibility, and introductions to each other. There is a specified process for incorporating the team into scope development and the development of work plans, etc. In addition, there are guidelines in place for project initiation team meetings, scheduled status reviews, business reviews, technical reviews, and a plan for regular and ongoing project reviews. These reviews should include the team, and will foster team buy-in. Regular status and progress meetings are conducted to keep project team members apprised of how the project is progressing, as well as to deal with issues that may arise. The project manager contributes to the performance evaluation of the individual team members. A rewards and recognition system is established whereby individual and team performance is acknowledged. A conflict management process is begun. Management enforces the process for team buy-in to ensure that teams are actively involved and integrated into scope planning and management of the project. A staff development plan is developed with the organization responsible for the professional development initiatives.

Professional Development

There is a general recognition within the organization that an individual's knowledge base, experience, and competence are contributing factors to the successful outcome of projects. As such, for large and highly visible projects there is an expectation that the project manager will have a fundamental knowledge set about project management and that the individual project team will be made aware of what is expected of them with regard to project management planning components. The organization now has a track record that documents the value of an individual's knowledge base, experience, and competence as significant contributing factors to the successful outcome of projects. As such, the organization expects that most individuals working on projects will understand how to apply the fundamentals (triple constraint) of the corporate project management process. In addition, the organization has begun to define different project-related roles.

Individual Project Management Knowledge
It is expected that project managers on large or highly visible projects will follow a defined process for attaining the triple constraint (scope-schedule-cost) and will be able to document and track these elements. It is also expected that individual project team members will understand what is expected of them in fulfilling these elements (such as contribution to scope validation, identification of schedule activities, and estimation of associated hours for completing schedule activities). Most individuals working on projects are expected to understand how to define the triple constraint elements of scope, schedule, and cost, and what is required for tracking

them. For large and highly visible projects it is
expected that the project managers will be able to
develop a complete project plan and manage to that
plan. Some individual project team members are
beginning to recognize project-related areas of
specialization, such as scheduling concepts,
budgeting concepts, project management
methodologies, etc.

Individual Project Management Experience/ Competence

It is expected that project managers on large or highly
visible projects have managed other projects in the
past successfully through proper control of project
outcomes, attaining a managed triple constraint and
positive customer evaluations. It is expected that
individual project team members have also had
successful experience working on other projects and
have demonstrated strong individual and teaming
attributes, as well as timely delivery of high-quality
deliverables. Most project managers within the
organization have been project managers on previous
projects and generally have a track record for
successfully completing projects within the triple
constraint parameters. Some individual project team
members are beginning to demonstrate project-
related specialties where they have strengths, such as
planner/scheduler, estimator, or methodologist.

Corporate Initiative for Project Management Development

The organization acknowledges that it is necessary to
have a defined project management process and has
made an educational course available to project
managers and project team members on large or

highly visible projects to educate them on how to utilize this defined process. In addition, there is a recognition process in place whereby those who are successful on large or highly visible projects will be acknowledged and compensated for their performance. The corporation makes available to anyone who will be involved on a project a project management essentials course, and all are encouraged to take this course to ensure a basic understanding of project management concepts and applicability. The organization is also beginning to define specific project-related roles that would be assigned to specific project team members. As such, the corporation recognizes that these separate roles will require different training, compensation, and motivation.

Level 3
Organizational Standards and Institutionalized Process

All projects are expected to follow the human resource planning process, which has been institutionalized. External stakeholders and customers are considered an integral part of the project team.

Human Resource Planning

A formal analysis is conducted to define the organizational, technical, and interpersonal interfaces that exist within the organization. Constraints that may be prevalent in attaining required resources — such as the type of organization, individual preferences to work on one project or another — are analyzed and a response is developed. There is a narrative description of the responsibilities for all of the project personnel.

Staff Acquisition

The project manager works with the project office and line manager in resource pool management and prioritization. The project manager may need to negotiate with line management for specific resources, or will have "preassigned" resources. On occasion the project manager may need to look outside the organization for specific expertise.

Develop and Manage Project Team

The project manager works with the project office and line management to establish collocation, as necessary. Project team peer evaluations may be conducted by the team for individual peer performance. A conflict management process has been developed and is being utilized on most projects. Management is integrally involved in the team buy-in process and a fully integrated project team includes the business unit, technical groups, strategic groups as necessary, the client, etc. All stakeholder input is fully solicited and is consciously incorporated into project planning and execution.

Professional Development

The organization has a defined project management process in place, and all project managers are expected to follow the process in planning and managing their projects. The organization has established different project-related roles and expects that the individuals who are pursuing a project-related career progression will complete a gap analysis defining their current project management knowledge and experience and their desired state, thus determining what their needs are.

Individual Project Management Knowledge

All project managers are expected to have a solid knowledge base about how to plan and track projects, including following the defined project management methodology of the organization, which addresses all knowledge areas. In addition, project managers are encouraged to pursue a relationship with a professional project management association and work toward a certificate or degree related to project management. Project team members who are interested in the profession of project management are encouraged to define an area of project specialty (or overall project management) and work toward attaining the knowledge required to fulfill that role.

Individual Project Management Experience/ Competence

Project managers are evaluated on their project performance, which includes their ability to meet the triple constraint parameters, customer satisfaction, and project team member satisfaction, to define a competency range that can be utilized for defining effectiveness. Project team members are actively pursuing the organizationally defined project roles and effectiveness measurements that are established to define competency in each of these roles. Client satisfaction surveys are periodically conducted to ascertain the abilities and impact of the project manager. This information is utilized to help determine competency and contributes to performance-related compensation.

Corporate Initiative for Project Management Development

The corporation insists that all project stakeholders (within the organization) attend a project management essentials course that covers the basic elements of project management and the specific roles and responsibilities of various project stakeholders (such as executive management or project sponsor). In addition, there are a series of project management courses geared toward the career progression of a project manager and there is at least one course for each of the recognized project team specialty areas. The organization recognizes that effective project management is a cornerstone to organizational success and that to create an environment for success the organization is responsible for defining project-related professional tracks. As such, the organization has defined different roles (and associated compensation, training, and motivation) within a project that are considered project team roles at or below the status of project manager: project manager, project controller, planner/scheduler, estimator, and project administrative support. Those who are interested in pursuing a career in a project-related discipline should have a gap analysis and game plan to gain the knowledge and skills required.

Level 4
Managed Process

All projects are expected to follow the human resource
planning process, which has been mandated. Management
expects the project managers, project office, and line
managers to work cohesively in resource pool management
and prioritization. Decisions relating to each project are
evaluated in light of other projects. Project team evaluations
and performance reporting for the individuals at the end of
the project play a significant role in individual performance
reviews and measurements. Project teams work in
conjunction with other corporate processes and systems.

Human Resource Planning

Project organizational planning is integrated into the
overall resource pool management and prioritization.
An action plan is developed to deal with the
organizational, technical, and interpersonal interfaces
that exist within the organization. Constraints to
resource planning are managed. There is commitment
by all stakeholders to the definition of the roles and
responsibilities in the staffing plan. Integrated
decision-making (which means that decisions are
evaluated based on their impact to both the project
and the organization) begins to occur.

Staff Acquisition

The project office has an effective resource pool
management (including skills inventory database)
and prioritization process in place that is used by the
line and project managers in fulfilling project
resource needs. Resource variance reports are
developed for all projects.

Develop and Manage Project Team

The organization adheres to a team development process to foster team concepts throughout the organization. A team development process is established by which teams on medium and large projects are expected to evolve. Team member training needs are identified and communicated to the project office and line management, who proactively works with the team member to meet those training needs. The project manager significantly contributes to the performance evaluation of the individual. The conflict management process is being utilized on all projects. The team buy-in process is engaged and used by the majority of projects. Management is actively engaged in the team — there is probably a project board in place that represents all stakeholders in the project. This project board is actively involved in the project on a regular basis (status, execution, planning, etc.).

Professional Development

Management supports the integration of the professional project-related tracks into the corporate human resource structure of the organization. Individuals are specifically hired based upon their project management knowledge and competence in the planning and execution of projects.

Individual Project Management Knowledge

Project managers on large or highly visible projects are expected to have a degree or PMP-type certificate. Project managers on small- or medium-size projects are encouraged to pursue a certificate, degree, or foundation set that demonstrates a solid knowledge base in project management. Project team members who have chosen to focus in a project-related specialty area are actively pursuing a related certificate or degree in that area.

Individual Project Management Experience/ Competence

A project-related role competency measurement has been defined and individuals are given a continuum that can be utilized for performance measurement and career growth. Client satisfaction surveys are periodically conducted to ascertain the abilities and impact of both the project manager and the project team members. This information is utilized to help determine competency and contributes to performance-related compensation.

Corporate Initiative for Project Management Development

The organization is actively staffing and providing a complete training curriculum for each of the different project-related roles from project manager to project sponsor to scheduler, etc. Additional project-related positions are defined by the organization for those who have the ability and interest to go beyond the general management of projects (thus are considered positions above that of project manager) to project management process expert, project management methodologist, and project management mentor/ advisor. A compensation package for each role is in place and is based upon performance measurements as defined in the role competency. Individuals are motivated based upon the career progression within the project management track, the incentives built into the system for successful project performance, and the customer satisfaction.

Level 5
Optimizing Process

An improvement procedure exists whereby the project management human resource planning processes and standards are periodically reviewed and enhancements are incorporated. Project teams identify and support improvements to the process. At the conclusion of each project, lessons learned are captured, evaluated, and incorporated into the process to improve the process and documentation. Management is actively involved in the resource management and prioritization process and reviews and supports improvements. Functional line management of other corporate processes and systems are aware, support, and involved in overall resource pool management and prioritization for projects and maintenance requirements. Resource pool management and the prioritization process are integrated such that management can see how resources are being utilized to ensure high productivity of resources. Project team evaluations and performance reporting contribute to overall project efficiency and effectiveness for enhanced resource utilization and corporate career path standards.

Human Resource Planning

Organizational planning is evaluated on a periodic basis and enhancements to the process are continuously incorporated. Performance metrics for human resources are utilized to define efficiency and effectiveness of resource utilization throughout the project. Stakeholder analysis effectiveness and efficiency is evaluated to ensure continuous involvement and sign-off throughout the project. Integrated decision-making (whereby all decisions are evaluated with regard to their impact on other projects) occurs in all projects. Lessons learned are captured for effective organizational planning.

Staff Acquisition

Enterprise resource forecasting is evaluated for continuous improvement and enhancements. The project manager resource requests are evaluated against the resource pool constraints and prioritization to ensure maximization of resource utilization in effectiveness and efficiency. Resource variance reports measure performance metrics of efficiency and effectiveness. Enterprise resource forecasting is being utilized. Lessons learned about the effectiveness of acquiring resources are captured.

Develop and Manage Project Team

The organization values investing in its people throughout the organization and actively ensures that project teams have all that is required to succeed on a regular basis. The question is continually asked (especially at project end): Are there ways in which we could get better team buy-in? This information is used to improve the overall process. Team member training needs are forecasted and acknowledged as value-added investment for the organization. Project conflict management process is integrated into the overall corporate management system and efficiency and effectiveness measurements are gathered. Team satisfaction is measured. Lessons learned about effective means of developing team synergy are captured.

Professional Development

Improvement procedures are in place and utilized. Lessons learned are regularly examined and used to improve documented processes. Projects are given high value within the organization; thus there is high visibility to the individuals who are actively involved in projects on a regular basis. Projects are directly tied to the success of the organization; thus there is a financial tie to success of the organization and the project-related positions that are responsible for successful project performance.

Individual Project Management Knowledge

An improvement process is in place to continuously improve the individual's knowledge base in project management. Lessons learned are captured and used to improve the monitoring and control efforts. All senior project-related personnel are either certified or degreed in their project specialty area and are serving as mentors/advisors to those who are pursuing a project-related career path. All nonsenior project-related personnel are actively pursuing a chosen project-related career path. Lessons learned about assessing individual project management knowledge are captured.

Individual Project Management Experience/ Competence

An improvement process is in place to continuously improve the individual's ability to attain experience and improve competency in project management. Lessons learned are captured and used to improve the monitoring and control efforts. All senior project-related personnel are seasoned professionals with multiple years of experience working successfully in their specialty area. Lessons learned about the application of project management knowledge to practical application are captured.

Corporate Initiative for Project Management Development

An improvement process is in place to continuously improve the organization's ability to enhance the project management professional track and opportunities. Lessons learned are captured and used to improve the monitoring and control efforts. The corporation supports and sponsors project manager- and team member-related certificate programs (such as requiring all project managers to be PMP® certified) and expects that individuals who define project management as their professional area complete the requisite corporate training curriculum. Senior project-related personnel are represented or involved in the executive corporate meetings and in defining the strategic direction of the organization. Lessons learned about the development of project personnel, turnover, and the correlation to successful project outcomes are captured.

CHAPTER 9

Project Communications Management

THE OVERALL PURPOSE of communications management is to manage the project data process from collection to categorization to dissemination to utilization and decision-making.

Components

Communications Planning

The purpose of communications planning is to determine the information and communications needs of all the project stakeholders, such as who, what, when, where, and how.

Information Distribution

This refers to the method or means of making information available to the project stakeholders, including retrieval and distribution systems.

Performance Reporting

This type of information is gathered and distributed during project execution and control and includes status reporting, progress measurement, and forecasting data, which are consolidated and analyzed reports received from project integration.

Issues Tracking and Management

What kind of issues-tracking and management processes are in place? Are they regularly used? Are issues really evaluated/prioritized or are they merely listed? Is there regular follow-up and reporting?

<u>Level 1</u>
Initial Process

There is an ad hoc communications process in place whereby projects are expected to provide informal status to management, when called upon to do so.

Communications Planning

There are no established standards in place for communications planning. However, it is expected that the project manager can provide a status on the project to management, when required.

Information Distribution

Information is distributed in an ad hoc manner, as a response to a specific request or question about the project directed to the project manager.

Performance Reporting

Informal reporting about the current status of the project can be obtained from the project manager.

Issues Tracking and Management

Issues are handled on an ad hoc basis and may be discussed in meetings.

Level 2
Structured Process and Standards

A basic communications management process is established whereby stakeholder communication needs and project constraints and assumptions are identified, project status and progress reporting are distributed on a regular basis, and there is a notification of phase and overall project completion. Large, highly visible projects are encouraged to follow the process and there is documentation supporting how the process should work. Management understands the need for regular communication of project activities in order to have the needed information to make good decisions and supports the collection of project status. The focus for communications is on summary status and progress reporting for the triple constraint items (scope-schedule-cost). Projects are launched through project requests from a client.

At this level the following activities (including components below) are required for large and highly visible projects, and encouraged for other projects:

- Applying the detailed communications management process, including analyzing the communications requirements and technology parameters

- Identifying the communication vehicles used to exchange information

- Baselining the project triple-constraint parameters.

Formal acceptance from the customer is obtained for project deliverables. The communications management process is fully documented and the process is repeatable. Communications templates exist and are readily accessible and integrated with other project planning elements. Management values the output of communications management and requires utilization of project management tools and techniques to communicate project outcomes and the triple constraint parameters.

Communications Planning

An informal stakeholder analysis is developed whereby project stakeholders are identified and provided project summary reports for status, progress, or phase completion. Project constraints and assumptions are developed. Management encourages large and highly visible projects to provide these summary reports at periodic intervals through the expected life of the project. A formal stakeholder analysis is conducted and communication requirements are defined by combining the type and format of information required with an analysis of the value of that information. A communications management plan is developed by large and highly visible projects and encouraged by all projects. The communication plan identifies the communication needs from project commencement to closure, including the post-project review at the end of the project, where lessons learned are gathered. The following communication technology factors are analyzed:

- Immediacy of the need for information
- Availability of technology
- Expected project staffing
- Length of the project
- Project risks.

Information Distribution

Information is distributed via either electronic
medium or hard-copy documentation (which is
hand-delivered or mailed to the stakeholders). Basic
retrieval and distribution process is in place. Effective
interteam communication retrieval of project actuals
is established. Project stakeholders are directed to a
specific shared file on a computer network or central
physical location, where they can retrieve needed
project information. The project manager is
responsible for ensuring that project information is
retrieved in a timely fashion and that the stakeholders
obtain the information that they need.

Performance Reporting

Three types of summary reports for status, progress
and phase completion can be produced throughout
the life of the project at periodic intervals of project
timeline. These reports track milestone attainment of
scheduled items. The project has been baselined and
actuals can be collected. The three consolidated
reports from integration (status reports, progress
reports, or phase project completion reports) contain
information about how many hours or dollars have
been spent on the project activities, how much of the
overall time has been spent on the project activities,
and the technical performance of the project. A
formal acceptance document is being used for the
customer to acknowledge acceptance of project
deliverables. At the conclusion of the project there is a
formal customer sign-off.

Issues Tracking and Management

There is a documented issues management process in
place, whereby issues are collected, documented,

managed, and brought to a conclusion. This process is followed at times and encouraged by large and highly visible projects, but is not enforced. Project deliverable completion and formal acceptance as well as project closure are reported. Not only is the issues management process in place, but it is consistently followed on large and highly visible projects. Management expects to be involved with the resolution of issues for large and highly visible projects, in the form of either notice or escalation, and also encourages involvement for other projects.

Level 3
Organizational Standards and Institutionalized Process

The communications management process has been institutionalized and a formal communications management plan is expected for most projects, including conducting informal variance/trend analysis. Management is actively involved in reviewing and acting upon communications reports from individual projects. Project performance reviews are conducted. Key management is involved in reviewing and approving any changes that impact the triple constraints.

Communications Planning

A communications plan is expected for all projects.

Information Distribution

There is a formal information retrieval system by which project stakeholders can retrieve information through an electronic text database or central repository (physical or electronic). There is a formal information distribution system including project meetings, hard copy documentation, shared access to networked electronic databases, fax, electronic mail, and voice mail. The project manager confirms stakeholder satisfaction with information dissemination on a regular basis.

Performance Reporting

Graphical performance reporting charts are used, such as S-curves (which indicate how the funds or hours are being spent), histograms, and tables, in addition to narrative reporting of project status and progress. In addition, informal variance/trend analysis can be conducted comparing the actual project results to the planned results, and trend analysis is done to determine the estimate-to-complete for budget and schedule parameters. At this stage the analysis is informal because the estimates and actuals do not result from close integration with other corporate systems.

Management is involved in the identification, analysis, approval (or not) of changes to the project plan. Performance reviews are conducted to assess project status or progress. Project reports are archived for future reference.

Issues Tracking and Management

Issues are consistently addressed during regular, full-team meetings. The client area is part of determining issues and coming up with proposed resolutions and actions.

Level 4
Managed Process

The communications management process is mandated for all projects and a formal communications management plan is expected for all projects, including formal variance/trend analysis. Project communications management plans are documented and integrated into the overall corporate communications structure.

Communications Planning

There is a method for updating and refining the communications management plan as the project progresses and develops and is incorporated into the corporate systems.

Information Distribution

There is an automated information retrieval system in place that is based upon a database structure and inquiry process. The information distribution system includes meetings of varying formats and also multimedia distribution, such as intranet, internet, and video conferencing. Project management confirms stakeholder access to and satisfaction with information dissemination system.

Performance Reporting

All projects are expected to capture performance measurements (such as earned value) for understanding and analysis of project performance. Formal variance/trend analysis is conducted on projects.

Issues Tracking and Management

The impacts of project issues to other areas of the organization are understood and project issues are prioritized for resolution and to minimize impact to the organization. Management receives regular reports on the number of issues that have been identified, their status, etc.

Level 5
Optimizing Process

An improvement process is in place to continuously improve project communications management. Lessons learned and improvements are documented into repeatable processes. Management is actively involved in project reviews and process enhancements. There is a project communications improvement procedure in place. Functional management is aware, supportive, and involved in project communications and uses the information to evaluate the impact of projects on functional operations. Efficiency and effectiveness metrics are incorporated into projects as part of defining value-added communications about project progress.

Communications Planning

Communications-planning documentation and lessons learned are analyzed for value-added impact. Communications planning is tightly linked with organizational planning. Lessons learned are collected about effective communications planning.

Information Distribution

Documentation of the entire project is available for review during administrative closure and lessons learned are evaluated to determine continuous quality improvement measurements of the process. Project stakeholders have been educated and are capable of accessing any project-related information that they need in a timely fashion. Lessons learned about effective information retrieval and distribution are collected.

Performance Reporting

Lessons learned are analyzed and the results are imbedded back into the process for continuous enhancements. Performance metrics are utilized to define efficiency and effectiveness metrics for projects. Lessons learned on all projects are captured for future reference.

Issues Tracking and Management

The issues tracking and management process is periodically evaluated to determine potential enhancements in the process. Issues are evaluated and prioritized based on their impact on project performance metrics of efficiency and effectiveness. Lessons learned about the effectiveness of the issues tracking and management process are collected.

CHAPTER 10

Project Risk Management

THE OVERALL PURPOSE of risk management is to identify, analyze, respond, and control risk factors throughout the life of a project. Risk management is understanding the risk events, assessing their impact on the project, determining the best way to deal with them, developing and executing a plan, and monitoring progress.

Components

Risk Identification

Risk identification involves determining which risks are likely to have an impact on the project and documenting the characteristics of each item. The main products of this component are potential risk events and risk triggers.

Risk Quantification

Risk quantification covers evaluating the risks and assessing the potential outcomes. Risk quantification includes examining all identified risks; determining the interactions, relationships, and implications to the project; developing probabilities of occurrence; determining which risks warrant response; and assessing the range of possible project outcomes. The main product is a prioritized list of quantified risk events.

Risk Response Development

Risk response involves defining the steps to managing the risks. It includes determining how best to respond and establish contingency plans, reserves, and agreements necessary to contain the risks. Planning strategies are developed to avoid, mitigate, or accept risks. Risk response includes the development of a risk management plan, project reserves, and mitigation strategies.

Risk Control

Risk control involves controlling risks, making decisions on how to handle each situation, and taking corrective action. Risk control is seeing a risk concern, deciding how to handle it, and carrying out the decision. Risks are controlled in accordance with the risk management plan and established procedures. The main products are a risk register, corrective actions, and updates to the risk management plan.

Risk Documentation

Risk documentation involves establishing a project database to collect historical information on the risks encountered and related experiences. The main products from this component include a historical database and postproject assessment.

<u>Level 1</u>
Initial Process

There is recognition of the need for accepted processes, but there are no established practices or standards. Individual teams or parts of the organization may have their own way of doing things in an ad hoc, informal fashion. Documentation of the processes is loose and makes it difficult to repeat the activities elsewhere. Management is aware that risk management has importance, but action in this area is more reactive than proactive.

Risk Identification

Risks are not identified as a normal practice. However, individuals may discuss items of special interest to management or stakeholders. However, these discussions typically take place when the risk is already a current problem versus a future possibility. To help identify risks, the project manager will generally have a scope statement and a WBS that consists of a basic set of milestones and occasionally deliverables. The project manager may also have a top-level milestone schedule. There may be sporadic "risk" discussions on the project scope and milestone information, but only on an ad hoc basis.

Risk Quantification

If risks are identified, the project manager may speculate on the impact to the project if the risks occur. The speculation is typically done in an impromptu situation without any analysis, forethought, or standard approach/process.

Risk Response Development

In large part, risks are considered as they arise. Teams seldom determine mitigation strategies or plan for contingencies for future risk events.

Risk Control

At this point, project teams do more day-to-day problem solving if a new risk event arises (developing workarounds) versus working with a risk management plan and identifying additional risk response strategies.

Risk Documentation

There is no historical database on typical risks encountered and related experiences. Individual team members rely upon their own past experiences and discussions with the project team.

<u>Level 2</u>
Structured Process and Standards

Risk management processes are developed and documented for identifying, quantifying, developing a risk response, and reporting risks. Project team members generally understand macro- and some detail-level risks, and most projects are expected to determine strategies for dealing with the risks. Teams use a structured approach to quantify the impact of the risks in an effort to rank their importance. Risk lists are compiled to track and monitor progress. The risk management processes are considered standard practice for large, visible projects, and recommended for all other projects. All documented processes are repeatable. Management supports risk management, but they are only consistently involved on large, visible projects and involved in other projects if the risk critical and is of great magnitude. Risks are examined and controlled on a project-by-project basis.

Risk Identification

The organization has a documented process for identifying project risks. The process is encouraged for all projects, but is only considered standard practice on large, highly visible projects. A conscious effort is made to identify total project risks (near-term and longer-term in as much detail as makes sense). Risk discussions include input from key stakeholders. To help identify risks, the project team will generally have a scope statement and a WBS template that goes down to at least level three, a more detailed project schedule, and a more comprehensive project cost estimate. The project team will also examine the procurement management plan and staff management plan to help identify risks. The risk discussions typically focus on project scope, schedule, and cost risks, and top-level risks are included in the project team project plan. The project team relies upon expert judgment and known industry lessons learned to identify risks.

Risk Quantification

A process is in place that is documented which provides a more structured approach to quantifying risks. The process includes a standard methodology that will ensure the organization consistently assesses the risk items. The common methodology may include low-medium-high ratings or expected monetary value of risks using simple probability and value calculations. Project teams attempt to employ more objective approaches to quantify the probability that a risk event will occur and the significance of the impact if it does occur. Risks are still evaluated on a project-by-project basis and are typically prioritized based upon a single factor such as monetary value considerations.

Risk Response Development

Project teams may informally think about their strategy for dealing with future risk events and discuss the strategies among themselves. The strategies may include avoiding the risk, mitigating it, or accepting it altogether. As part of the risk management process, the organization has the project teams develop a risk management plan that documents the procedures that will be used to manage risk. The plan will cover things such as who is responsible, how the information will be maintained, how plans will be implemented, and how reserves will be distributed. The plan is provided for integration and consolidation into the project plan. Large, highly visible projects are developing contingency plans for near-term risks and mitigation strategies for all risk areas of concern.

Risk Control

During project execution, individual project teams and segments of the organization apply their own approach to managing and controlling risks. Project teams typically assign responsibility for each risk item as it occurs. That responsibility may include providing a recommendation about how to handle the risk and taking corrective action. Risks may be discussed in team staff meetings and the status is documented in meeting minutes. Management is generally informed about the risk status of large, highly visible projects. A process is developed and documented to report risk status to key stakeholders. The process may include a risk log/register that identifies the risk items, who is responsible, the potential impact, the probability of impact, the mitigation strategy, and the current status. Project teams may hold periodic meetings specifically for risk discussions to track and manage the risks and to discuss current status, workarounds, and corrective actions, as needed. The organization collects metrics to track things such as the number of risk items and levels of concern (e.g., high, medium, low). The risk status is distributed to key stakeholders and incorporated into the project schedule.

172 Risk Documentation

Individuals may have collected some "historical" information about general tendencies in risk, but the information is not typically collected and centralized. The organization process includes the establishment of a historical database to collect risk information such as typical risks on similar projects.

Level 3
Organizational Standards and Institutionalized Process

The risk processes are considered an organizational standard and are being utilized by nearly all projects. The risk identification process is expanded to include efficient ways for teams to identify risks (e.g., checklists, automated forms, etc.). In addition, teams are asked to identify symptoms of risk (risk triggers) for incorporation into the historical database. The risk quantification process is expanded to identify more advanced procedures for quantifying risks and multiple criteria to prioritize risk items. The risk response development process is enhanced with templates. All processes are repeatable. A risk control system is developed and established. Systems are becoming more integrated: risk information and status is provided to project integration. Metrics are collected and analyzed, such as the types of risks and success rate in mitigating the items. Management fully supports the risk management processes and has institutionalized the procedures and standards. Risks are examined and controlled on a program basis.

Risk Identification

The organization has a documented, repeatable process for identifying project risks, which is fully implemented. Documentation exists on all processes and standards for identifying risk events. The process is expanded to include efficient avenues for teams to identify risks (e.g., checklists, automated forms, etc.). In addition, teams are to identify symptoms of risk (risk triggers) for incorporation into the historical database for risks. A conscious effort is made to identify total project risks and program risks (interrelationships among related projects). Risk discussions include input from past, similar projects, industry lessons learned, and key stakeholders. Risk information and symptoms are consolidated and integrated.

Risk Quantification

The risk quantification process is further expanded to identify more advanced procedures for quantifying risks and multiple criteria to prioritize risk items. The entire process is fully documented and repeatable. The more advanced process may include methodologies such as range predictions, optimal calculations using simulation tools and decision trees, and weighted average calculations. Risks are typically prioritized using multiple factors such as expected monetary value, criticality, timing, and risk type. Risks are evaluated on a program/organizational basis.

Risk Response Development

The risk response development process is expanded to include templates for the risk management plan. At this point, the project teams typically have contingency plans and mitigation strategies identified for each risk item. Consequently, the organization is capable of allocating project reserves to cover such items.

Risk Control

A process is fully developed and utilized for managing and controlling risk. Project risks are actively, routinely tracked. Corrective actions are taken, the risk management plan is updated as risk events take place and/or things change, and project plans are adjusted accordingly. Metrics are collected, analyzed, and may be expanded to include success rate at mitigating risks.

Risk Documentation

The organization is collecting historical information such as common risk items and risk triggers and organizing the information in the historical database.

Level 4
Managed Process

All processes are in place, documented, and being utilized by nearly all projects. Processes and standards are integrated with other corporate processes and systems. Integration management includes the risk management process with the project office, cost management, time management, finance/accounting, and strategic planning processes. There is a mandate to comply with the organizational risk management processes and procedures. Management takes an "organizational view" of projects.

Risk Identification

All processes are in place, documented, and being utilized. The risk identification process is fully integrated with cost management and time management processes, and the project office. A conscious effort is made to identify total project risks: within individual projects, within programs, and between projects/programs. In other words, risks are identified with the organization and project in mind.

Risk Quantification

All processes are in place, documented, and being utilized. The risk quantification process is fully integrated with cost management, time management, finance/accounting, and strategic planning processes, and the project office. Risk quantification now takes into effect the risks on other projects and other parts of the organization. Risks are evaluated on an organizational basis. As appropriate, performance indices are included in calculating the impact of risk on a project.

Risk Response Development

All processes are in place, documented, and being utilized. The risk response development process is fully integrated with cost management, time management, finance/accounting, and strategic planning processes, and the project office.

Risk Control

All processes are in place, documented, and being utilized. The risk control system is integrated with the organization's control systems, monitoring programs, cost management, and time management processes.

Risk Documentation

The historical database is expanded to include common interdependency risks between projects.

Project Management Maturity Model

178

Level 5
Optimizing Process

Improvement procedures are in place and utilized. Lessons learned are regularly examined and used to improve documented processes. Projects are managed with consideration of how similar projects performed in the past and what is expected for the future. Management uses efficiency and effectiveness metrics to make decisions regarding the project. All projects, changes, and issues are evaluated based upon metrics from cost estimates, baseline estimates, and earned value. The metrics are used to understand the performance of a project during execution for making management decisions for the future.

Risk Identification

An improvement process is in place to continuously improve risk identification to completely identify all risks as early as possible. Lessons learned are captured and used to improve risk identification activity. The risk identification process includes a method to identify an organizational priority for the project. The priority designator is linked to the management decisions and gives project teams the ability to identify the priority of their risk concerns. The enhanced process is developed, documented, and in place. Lessons learned are being captured.

Risk Quantification

An improvement process is in place to continuously improve risk quantification to better quantify risks and adequately capture the cost and schedule impact. Lessons learned are captured and used to improve risk quantification efforts. Management uses the quantified risks to make decisions regarding the project. A process utilizing absolute values of risk for making management decisions before and during project execution is developed, documented, and in place. Lessons learned are being captured.

Risk Response Development

An improvement process is in place to continuously improve the risk response development process and development of the risk management plan. Lessons learned are captured and used to improve the development effort of identifying risk strategies. Use of project reserves is included in the determination of project efficiency and effectiveness. A process for tracking the use of project reserves is in place and supports management decisions during project execution. Lessons learned are being captured.

Risk Control

An improvement process is in place to continuously improve the risk control process. Lessons learned are captured and used to improve the monitoring and control efforts. Risk assessments are incorporated and included in the determination of project efficiency and effectiveness. A process utilizing risk assessments and the current risk status for management decisions during project execution is developed, documented, and in place. Lessons learned are being captured.

Risk Documentation

An improvement process is in place to continuously improve the risk documentation process and historical database. Lessons learned are captured and used to improve the collection activity. Postproject assessments are conducted and lessons learned are captured in the historical database.

CHAPTER 11

Project Procurement Management

PROCUREMENT MANAGEMENT IS the processes and actions undertaken by the project manager and/or project team to acquire goods and services in support of the project. It also includes activities in managing the contract throughout the period of performance and closing the contract upon completion. Procurement planning involves planning for all purchases, acquisitions and contracting. All these processes and actions must be taken within the constraints of the organizational structure and policies of the overall organization. Generally the process involves contracting with an outside vendor to acquire goods and services in a timely manner, in the appropriate quantity, and within a defined quality standard. In fact, the term "contracting" is often used interchangeably with "procurement."

Components

Procurement Planning

Procurement planning involves determining whether to procure or produce in-house, deciding how to procure, identifying what and how much to procure, and determining when to procure. If any goods or services are to be acquired from outside the project team, the specifications should be laid out in detail, along with the major milestones, timing/scheduling, initial cost estimate, and budget impact. The outcome of this component is the procurement management plan.

Requisition

Requisition bridges the gap between identifying requirements and contracting with the outside world. The process of planning to contract includes identifying potential vendors, determining solicitation type (oral or verbal, invitation for bid, request for proposal, etc.), determining the type of contract, developing procurement documents, etc. The outcome of this component is a solicitation package.

Solicitation/Source Selection

This process involves finding the right vendor and negotiating the contract for goods and services. It includes soliciting information from industry, receiving the bids/proposals, evaluating the information, negotiating the contract, and finalizing the contract award. The outcome of this component is the award of the contract.

Contract Management/Closure

This includes actions involved with vendor management during contract performance, acceptance by the client, payment for services, and close-out activities. The purpose is to assure that the seller performs in accordance with the terms of the contract and receives proper reimbursement (in both quantity and timing).

Level 1
Initial Process

There is no project procurement process in place, but the organization does recognize that there may be value in having a defined procurement process. Some project managers recognize the need to go through the process of procuring outside goods and services in a methodical manner, although these methods are ad hoc and inconsistently performed. Contracts are managed at a final delivery level.

Procurement Planning

There is no recognized practice for procurement planning within a project. However, occasionally (on an ad hoc basis) a project manager will determine basic requirements and timing from the milestones and deliverables list and will then plot out a planned approach to purchasing goods and services ahead of time.

Requisition

Basically, project requisitions are prepared in a manner similar to the way the organization prepares documentation to acquire more typical goods and services. There is no uniquely established approach for making acquisitions for projects.

Solicitation/Source Selection

There is no standard or practice in place for vendor contact/evaluation/negotiation. Occasionally the organization will go through a process of contacting several vendors, shopping and comparing prices.

184 **Contract Management/Closure**

Contracts for projects are loosely managed with minimal reporting requirements delineated within the contract. In large part, vendors/contractors are managed to end dates only.

Level 2
Structured Process and Standards

There is a basic process documented for procurement of goods and services from outside the organization, but this process is not a standard practice. Its use by large or highly visible projects is encouraged. The procurement organization drives the process with some input from the project team, organizational management, and the client. The process for procurement is considered standard practice for large, highly visible projects, and all other projects are encouraged to use it. The process is specific and documented. Organizational management is more involved, with input from the client department. The process involves the project team and capitalizes upon its technical knowledge. Contracts are managed at an appropriate level of detail with regular periodic reporting.

Procurement Planning

The basic process specifies that the project manager decides whether to make or buy the goods/services in question after receiving a project request. This is done in the process of creating a statement of work/ product description. This statement of work/product description is sent to the scope management process, which prepares and returns a scope statement. The project manager (and possibly team members) go through an informal analysis whether to "make or buy" the goods and services in question with input from the client department. This analysis is heavily based upon the scope statement. They make a recommendation to organizational management. In the case where organizational management makes the decision to proceed with buying goods/services, the procurement organization and the project team jointly create the procurement management plan. This plan identifies items such as how to procure, what, how much, when, what deliverables the quality necessary for these deliverables (based upon the project's quality standards), and timing for these deliverables.

Requisition

This scope statement is reviewed (changed if necessary), and if the decision is to build the product internally, a scope approval is returned to the scope management process. If the decision is to buy the goods/services in question from an outside vendor, the procurement organization takes the lead on deciding which vendor(s) to contact. The procurement organization also takes the lead on preparing the procurement documentation with limited participation from the project team. The project team becomes more involved in the preparation of the procurement documentation. A process is defined for identifying contract requirements, identifying potential vendors, selecting the appropriate contract type, determining the best procurement approach, and developing procurement documentation. The organization establishes clear evaluation criteria for use during proposal evaluation.

The procurement approach will vary, but the organization has defined the different types for use by the project teams:

Unilateral

• Purchase Order (PO) — usually is used when routine, standard cost items are needed. Sent to the seller with the expectation that it will accept it automatically.

Bilateral

- Request for Quotation (RFQ) — usually used when the goods and services are of relatively low dollar value, such as supplies and materials.

- Request for Proposal (RFP) — usually used when there is a high dollar value involved and the goods and services are not standardized. This would be when the project team has developed the requirements for the product, but has not done a detailed design of the product.

- Invitation to Bid — usually used for high-dollar-value, "standard" goods and services. Use of this approach depends upon a clear and accurate description of the goods and services; in other words, the project team must have a thoroughly documented design of the product, which will be conveyed to the potential vendor(s).

Large, highly visible projects use the process to obtain contract services for projects.

Solicitation/Source Selection

Usually, the procurement organization contacts the vendor(s) and conducts price comparisons. The vendor(s) is asked to commit to the final delivery date for the services with key milestones. No specific quality standards are detailed for the vendor. The vendor(s) is asked for a project plan at an appropriate level of detail. The quality to be met in the product is specified to the vendor, based upon the project's quality standards. Both the project manager and the purchasing department are involved in the evaluation of the bids/proposals, using the established evaluation criteria. A process is defined to solicit information from industry, evaluate the information, negotiate the contract, and finalize contract award. The process is used on large, highly visible projects.

Contract Management/Closure

The vendor is expected to supply to the project manager periodic status reports that reflect progress toward meeting key milestones; no specific format or frequency has been specified in the basic process. Changes to the plan may represent a scope change, in which case the normal change management process within the project integration process is used for large, highly visible projects.

Formal acceptance and contract closure occurs, but a standard process is not established or documented. The vendor reports on a regular basis (usually weekly) on the reporting level agreed upon in the contract. The format of this reporting is specified in the procurement process, and the reporting frequency is per the procurement management plan and contract. Information on work results is provided to the project integration management process for internal progress reporting. In the case where there is a change to the plan (e.g., date slippage), the project manager sends corrective action information to the project integration management process, resulting in plan updates.

Corrective action information and other changes are sent to the project integration management process, resulting in project plan updates or use of the change control process within the project integration process.

A process is established and documented for formal acceptance and contract closure. Typically closure information and formal acceptance is provided to the communication process.

Level 3
Organizational Standards and Institutionalized Process

The procurement process is considered an organizational standard, and is used by nearly all projects. The client is directly and integrally involved in the analysis and decision to make or buy. The procurement is run with a much more program view — that is, management views other projects and products in the program in making their decisions. The project team and purchasing department are now fully integrated in the procurement process. Contractors/vendors are asked to comply with applicable project management processes and structure that are standard throughout the organization.

Procurement Planning

The project team and procurement organization present a formal analysis/recommendation report to both organizational management and client management. The make/buy recommendation and decision takes into account effects and ramifications in such areas as capacity of the organization, most economical method, economic factors, organization situations, etc. The make/buy decision is made jointly by organizational management and client management.

Requisition

The organization has developed an expeditious process to access vendors/contractors (for example, a preferred bidders list). Any vendor recommendations from the project team should come from, or be added to, this list. The process for developing procurement documentation is expanded to include procurement templates such as a statement of work format, status reporting, and other common procurement attachments. The organization has identified the types of contracts. These processes and lists are incorporated into the project's Procurement Management Plan.

The type of contract will vary, but the organization has defined the different types for use by the project teams:

- Firm-fixed-price — used when reasonably definite product specifications are available and costs are relatively certain. The team has done a detailed job of designing the product.
- Fixed-price-plus-incentive-fee — used when the contract is for a substantial sum and involves a long delivery period.
- Cost-plus-incentive-fee — used when the contract involves a long delivery period with substantial amount of hardware development and test requirements.
- Cost-plus-fixed-fee — used primarily for research projects where the effort required for successful completion is uncertain until well after the signing of the contract.
- Cost-plus-percentage-of-cost — rarely used.

Solicitation/Source Selection

Contractors/vendors are asked to comply with applicable project management processes and structure that is standard throughout the organization. Vendors are asked to supply a detailed plan, including a WBS and detailed, sequenced activity list, in line with the project's structure.

Solicitation is carried out jointly by the purchasing department and the project team, with input from the legal department. Techniques such as Seller Rating Systems and Proposal Evaluation Criteria are established and used consistently.

Contract Management/Closure

The vendor reports in a timely manner (generally weekly or monthly depending upon the length of the project and frequency of contract deliverables) to the project manager against progress on the detailed sequenced activity list. Any changes/issues are communicated immediately to the project manager, who forwards them to the change management process, which is fully implemented within the project.

The client is integrally involved in testing of the product and signs off on contract completion. After the client has signed off on the acceptability of the procured items, and all appropriate documentation from the vendor has been received, the project manager signs off on the contract and closure actions take place.

Level 4
Managed Process

Organizational management now mandates compliance with the procurement process for all projects. Make/buy decisions are now made with an organizational perspective. The vendor is integrated into the organization's reporting mechanisms. Audits of the procurement process are performed to provide insight into how procurement actions may be improved.

Procurement Planning

The make/buy decision is made by a team composed of the project manager, organizational management, client management, and the purchasing department. This decision includes organizational factors such as available production capacity in other parts of the organization, ramifications on other active projects, ramifications on other parts of the organizational environment, etc. Input is requested from all areas affected by the project or its product(s).

Requisition

The project's requisitions are fully integrated with the organization's requisition process.

Solicitation/Source Selection

Solicitation and source selection for the project are fully integrated with the organization's solicitation process. In this manner, it is possible for the organization to leverage numerous requests to a given vendor and take advantage of economies of scale.

Contract Management/Closure

The vendor is required to report progress against plan using the organization's standard project management tools and techniques. Weekly status reports are provided from the vendor to the project manager, who integrates them into the organization's standard status reporting mechanisms. In addition, vendors are more integrated into the project planning activities.

Level 5
Optimizing Process

An improvement procedure exists whereby the project management procurement processes and standards are periodically reviewed and enhancements are incorporated. The project manager and project teams identify and support improvements to the process. At the conclusion of each project, lessons learned are captured, evaluated, and incorporated into the process to improve the process and documentation. The procurement process is evaluated based upon efficiency and effectiveness metrics. Management is actively involved in obtaining strategic alliances with approved vendors who have a reputation for delivering high-quality products or services in a timely manner and supports improvements to the process for just-in-time delivery.

Procurement Planning

Procurement planning is evaluated on a periodic basis, and enhancements to the process are continuously incorporated. The make/buy decision is evaluated based upon efficiency and effectiveness metrics. Historical data about projected make/buy costs are evaluated against actual costs to determine if the decisions were sound and should be repeated in the future. Just-in-time procurement is incorporated to expedite the procurement planning process and reduce inventory carrying costs for the organization.

Requisition

The requisition process is evaluated on a periodic basis and enhancements to the process are continuously incorporated. The requisition process is automated and triggered by a project manager request. The process is evaluated based upon efficiency and effectiveness metrics. The organization has preferred contract vehicles and a list of preferred vendors who can respond to the requisition process expeditiously.

Solicitation/Source Selection

Solicitation/source selection is evaluated on a periodic basis and enhancements to the process are continuously incorporated. Contractors are evaluated based upon effectiveness and efficiency metrics with regard to project performance. The project manager and project team evaluate the vendors at the end of the project in terms of effectiveness, efficiency, responsiveness, timeliness, and quality of product/ service. The results of these evaluations are fed back into the process and measured against the preferred providers list.

Contract Management/Closure

Contract management/closure is evaluated on a periodic basis and enhancements to the process are continuously incorporated. The organization considers strategic alliances with preferred vendors. Both organizations adhere to a high standard of project performance and quality in their products or services. Captured on large and highly visible projects are lessons learned about the procurement process within the project with regard to effectiveness and efficiency (e.g., processing procurement documentation, having evaluation criteria to select a source, and the length of time to process a change order). A performance database exists to capture performance information on the vendors/contractors.

Appendices

Self-Assessment Survey

THIS SELF-ASSESSMENT survey is designed to help you perform a simple, informal self-assessment of your organization's project management maturity. More detailed information about assessments and how to use them is found in Chapter 1. Follow the directions below to perform your self-assessment. Remember that the primary purpose of a project management maturity assessment is to provide a path for your organization to move forward in improving its project management capabilities.

To Assess Your Organization's Project Management Maturity:

- Review the description for each component in each of the nine knowledge areas (see Chapters 2–11), and assess your level of maturity. Check the appropriate boxes in the survey.

- Achievement of a given maturity level by an organization is *cumulative* — that is, for each succeeding PMMM Level, the assumption is that all criteria for the preceding levels for that component are being (or have been) fulfilled. So for you to assess yourself at Level 3 in Scope Definition, for example, you must have in place all of the processes described in Levels 1, 2, and 3 of Scope Definition. You may have some of the processes in place in Level 4, but if you don't have all of those processes in place, you are at Level 3.

- After you have completed your assessment of the knowledge area components, determine your maturity level in each knowledge area. To do that, review your assessments of the knowledge area components, and pick the lowest level that you've assessed yourself — that is your level of maturity in that knowledge area. For example, if your component self-assessment is as shown in Figure A.1, then your maturity

200

	1	2	3	4	5
Project Scope Management					
Scope Planning and Management	☐	☑	☐	☐	☐
Requirements Definition (Business)	☐	☐	☑	☐	☐
Requirements Definition (Technical)	☐	☐	☑	☐	☐
Work Breakdown Structure	☐	☐	☑	☐	☐
Scope Change Control	☐	☐	☑	☐	☐

Project Management Maturity Level

Figure A.1. Sample self-assessment for project scope management. This organization is at Level 2 maturity in scope management.

level in project scope management is Level 2 (because you are at Level 2 maturity in business requirements definition).

- To assess your overall Organizational Maturity Level, follow a similar method. Review your maturity assessment of each of the nine knowledge areas. Pick the lowest level that you've assessed yourself — that is your Organizational Maturity Level. For example, if your knowledge area self-assessment is as shown in Figure A.2, then your overall Organizational Maturity Level is Level 1.

	1	2	3	4	5
Knowledge Area Maturity Level					
Project Integration Management	☐	☑	☐	☐	☐
Project Scope Management	☐	☑	☐	☐	☐
Project Risk Management	☐	☐	☑	☐	☐
Project Procurement Management	☑	☐	☐	☐	☐

Project Management Maturity Level

Figure A.2. This organization is at Organizational Maturity Level 1 (because it is at Level 1 in risk management).

PMMM Self-Assessment Survey Checklist

	Project Management Maturity Levels				
	1	2	3	4	5
Project Integration Management					
Deliverables Identification	☐	☐	☐	☐	☐
Scope Definition	☐	☐	☐	☐	☐
Project Management Plan Development	☐	☐	☐	☐	☐
Project Management Plan Execution	☐	☐	☐	☐	☐
Change Control	☐	☐	☐	☐	☐
Project Closure	☐	☐	☐	☐	☐
Project Information System	☐	☐	☐	☐	☐
Project Office	☐	☐	☐	☐	☐
Project Scope Management					
Scope Planning and Management	☐	☐	☐	☐	☐
Requirements Definition (Business)	☐	☐	☐	☐	☐
Requirements Definition (Technical)	☐	☐	☐	☐	☐
Work Breakdown Structure	☐	☐	☐	☐	☐
Scope Change Control	☐	☐	☐	☐	☐
Project Time Management					
Activity and Resource Definition	☐	☐	☐	☐	☐
Activity Sequencing	☐	☐	☐	☐	☐
Schedule Development	☐	☐	☐	☐	☐
Schedule Control	☐	☐	☐	☐	☐
Schedule Integration	☐	☐	☐	☐	☐
Project Cost Management					
Cost Estimating	☐	☐	☐	☐	☐
Cost Budgeting	☐	☐	☐	☐	☐
Performance Measurement	☐	☐	☐	☐	☐
Cost Control	☐	☐	☐	☐	☐
Project Quality Management					
Quality Planning	☐	☐	☐	☐	☐
Quality Assurance	☐	☐	☐	☐	☐
Quality Control	☐	☐	☐	☐	☐
Management Oversight	☐	☐	☐	☐	☐

	Project Management Maturity Levels				
	1	2	3	4	5
Project Human Resource Management					
Human Resource Planning	☐	☐	☐	☐	☐
Staff Acquisition	☐	☐	☐	☐	☐
Develop and Manage Project Team	☐	☐	☐	☐	☐
Professional Development	☐	☐	☐	☐	☐
Project Communications Management					
Communications Planning	☐	☐	☐	☐	☐
Information Distribution	☐	☐	☐	☐	☐
Performance Reporting	☐	☐	☐	☐	☐
Issues Tracking and Management	☐	☐	☐	☐	☐
Project Risk Management					
Risk Identification	☐	☐	☐	☐	☐
Risk Quantification	☐	☐	☐	☐	☐
Risk Response Development	☐	☐	☐	☐	☐
Risk Control	☐	☐	☐	☐	☐
Risk Documentation	☐	☐	☐	☐	☐
Project Procurement Management					
Procurement Planning	☐	☐	☐	☐	☐
Requisition	☐	☐	☐	☐	☐
Solicitation/Source Control	☐	☐	☐	☐	☐
Contract Management/Closure	☐	☐	☐	☐	☐
KNOWLEDGE AREA MATURITY LEVEL					
Project Integration Management	☐	☐	☐	☐	☐
Project Scope Management	☐	☐	☐	☐	☐
Project Time Management	☐	☐	☐	☐	☐
Project Cost Management	☐	☐	☐	☐	☐
Project Quality Management	☐	☐	☐	☐	☐
Project Human Resource Management	☐	☐	☐	☐	☐
Project Communications Management	☐	☐	☐	☐	☐
Project Risk Management	☐	☐	☐	☐	☐
Project Procurement Management	☐	☐	☐	☐	☐
ORGANIZATIONAL MATURITY LEVEL	☐	☐	☐	☐	☐

Second Edition Changes

These notes document the changes made to the first edition of the *Project Management Maturity Model,* primarily to reflect changes related to the release of the Project Management Institute's *A Guide to the Project Management Body of Knowledge Third Edition (PMBOK® Guide).*

General Changes

• There are slight changes to Chapters 1 and 2, due to SEI's change from SW-CMM and SE-CMM to CMMI. Also the Project Scope Management knowledge area now has five components as opposed to six in previous versions.
• "Risk Log" is changed to "Risk Register."
• "Project Plan" is changed to "Project Management Plan."
• All references to Executing/Controlling are updated to Executing/Monitoring/Controlling.

Chapter 3 — Project Integration Management

• Initiation and Close are now part of Project Integration Management.
• Initiation and Scope Definition is an added component that refers to Project Charter development and Preliminary Project Scope Statement development.
• Deliverables Identification is added as a component of Project Integration Management. Emphasis is placed on precise description of deliverables/scope. Deliverables and the WBS are closely tied together.

• Project Closure is added as a component of Project Integration Management. Wording is added to reflect review and acceptance of documents, drawings and hardware, as opposed to just software-related testing, acceptance and closure.

Chapter 4 — Project Scope Management

• Scope Planning and Management is an added component that calls for the development of a Scope Management Plan.

• Deliverables Identification and Scope Definition components have been removed, (the content was moved to Project Integration Management).

Chapter 5 — Project Time Management

• "Activity Definition" is changed to "Activity and Resource Definition." Types and quantities of resources are defined when activities are identified and defined.

Chapter 6 — Project Cost Management

• The Resource Planning component is removed from Project Cost Management (resources are identified in the Project Time Management knowledge area now).

Chapter 7 — Project Quality Management

• References to documents, drawings and hardware are added to the Quality Control Component, rather than maintaining an IT or software development only view of QC.

Chapter 8 — Project Human Resource Management

• "Organizational Planning" is renamed "Human Resource Planning" and "Team Development and Buy-In" is renamed "Develop and Manage Project Team."

• "Staffing Plan" is now "Staffing Management Plan."

Project Portfolio Management Maturity Model

Enhancing an organization's portfolio management capabilities is an important piece of its overall project management maturity. PM Solutions' Project Portfolio Management Maturity Model is built around six essential components of portfolio management. The model is patterned after the Software Engineering Institute's Capability Maturity Models. It has five distinct levels of maturity and examines an organization's implementation across the six project portfolio management components (see Figure A.3). We identified six components essential to developing an effective organizational portfolio management environment.

Portfolio Governance

This component addresses processes that facilitate the governance of an organization's project portfolio.

Fundamental Areas of Focus

- Portfolio governance process
- Initial consideration of alignment to the organization's vision, strategy, or objectives supported by basic alignment criteria
- Portfolio review board operations (policies and procedures)

- Portfolio review board membership (balance of project management and business knowledge)
- Portfolio review board charting process for establishing division-level portfolio review boards

As the Organization Matures within this Component...
Portfolio governance processes, procedures, and decision-making evolve as an enterprise portfolio review board is established to compliment the division-level portfolio review boards. The portfolio is managed against strategic criteria, and balanced to maintain an optimal mix of projects to achieve the organization's strategies.

Project Opportunity Assessment
This component addresses the processes around identifying and consistently assessing project opportunities.

Fundamental Areas of Focus
- Project opportunity identification/assessment process
- Roles and responsibilities
- Business value determination
- Portfolio review board

As the Organization Matures within this Component...
Processes such as opportunity identification, business case development, project approval, post-implementation project review and lessons learned are refined and consistently applied across the enterprise. Project portfolio management processes are continually assessed and improved with a particular emphasis on supporting management decision-making during opportunity assessment activities. The portfolio review board becomes more active in the analysis of cost-benefit, schedule, and risk data. Post-implementation reviews validate actual results for comparison to initial data and the information is used for process improvement efforts.

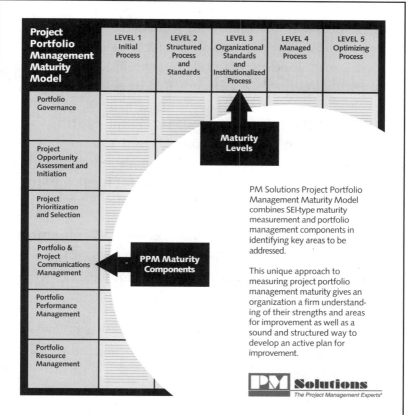

Figure A.3. PM Solutions' Project Portfolio Management Maturity Model covers five distinct levels of maturity, similar to those of the SEI CMMs, across six project portfolio management components.

Project Prioritization and Selection

This component addresses processes that facilitate the review, prioritization, and selection of projects in the project portfolio.

Fundamental Areas of Focus

• Project prioritization processes and criteria

• Selection and funding process

• Portfolio review board

As the Organization Matures within this Component...
Prioritization becomes more consistent across the
organization as the processes and criteria become better
defined, understood, consistently interpreted, and applied.
The portfolio review board becomes more active in the
review and selection process at the division level, evolving to
the enterprise level. An established process supports
executive decision-making concerning new project
proposals. Portfolio development information is collected
and maintained, including baseline data for the portfolio
management processes.

Portfolio and Project Communications Management
This component addresses processes that facilitate the
collection and sharing of portfolio information.

Fundamental Areas of Focus
- List of approved projects (beginning at the division level)
- Portfolio information defined (consistent set of data for
  each project)
- Portfolio information shared across the division
- Processes for sharing information
- Project management processes
- Categorization of projects and balancing of project
  investment with organizational goals

As the Organization Matures within this Component...
Adherence to corporate project management processes –
initially at the division level, then at the enterprise-level –
enable the enhancement of the project portfolio list or
database. The project list or database covers the entire
organization and portfolio information is available to all
divisions for their use as they participate in the organization's
project management and portfolio management processes.
Project investment information is readily available.

Portfolio Performance Management

This component addresses processes that facilitate the collection, analysis, and management of information used in portfolio performance management processes and decision-making.

Fundamental Areas of Focus

- Portfolio performance management process
- Portfolio review with sponsors and other key stakeholders
- Portfolio information sharing with sponsors and other key stakeholders
- Portfolio review board

As the Organization Matures within this Component...
Processes and standards guiding portfolio performance management are institutionalized, portfolio reviews are conducted regularly, and portfolio analysis is conducted to ensure the appropriate balance of project investments. The portfolio review board operates at the enterprise level and provides project oversight through regular portfolio progress reviews. The enterprise portfolio review board prioritizes projects using defined criteria. There is an emphasis on maintaining the performance of a balanced portfolio – monitoring the actual progress and delivery projects against their investment and planned benefit.

Portfolio Resource Management

This component addresses processes that facilitate the assignment of resources across the organization to support the projects in the organization's portfolio.

Fundamental Areas of Focus

- Resource assignment process
- Skills identification at the division-level

- Project prioritization and resource assignment across the division (based on skills and availability)
- Cross-divisional resource assignment is coordinated to support prioritized projects

As the Organization Matures within this Component...
Project prioritization is conducted at the enterprise-level by the portfolio review board. Portfolio resource management functions are executed with an enterprise perspective. Resource assignment is based upon resource skills, prioritization, and project priorities. Resource pools are managed and contain all types of resources. The enterprise portfolio review board oversees the portfolio to ensure resource continuity across projects.

The Portfolio Management Maturity Model examines each of these six components independently against the criteria for each of the five levels of maturity.

Levels of Project Portfolio Management Maturity

The Project Portfolio Management Maturity Model developed by PM Solutions is patterned after the SEI CMMs. The five levels of the model are described below. Each level represents a discrete organizational capability. The Portfolio Management Maturity Model examines each level within the six project portfolio management components.

LEVEL 1
Initial Process

- No processes or only ad hoc processes exist
- Portfolio information not readily available
- Roles and responsibilities not understood
- No project or resource inventories

LEVEL 2
Structured Process and Standards

- Basic processes exist
- Business value of projects understood
- Mix of intermediate and summary-level information
- Portfolio reviewed periodically
- Simple prioritization scheme established at division-level
- Roles and responsibilities defined
- Basic project and resource inventories exists

LEVEL 3
Organizational Standards
and Institutionalized Process

- Organization-wide processes standard
- Summary and *detailed* information available
- Enterprise-wide portfolio actively analyzed and monitored
- Project strategy aligned with business strategy
- Processes integrated with corporate processes
- Roles and responsibilities defined, linked to business value

LEVEL 4
Managed Process

- Post-implementation reviews using quantitative and qualitative data
- Repository of portfolio development information established, updated, and maintained
- Project portfolio information is audited
- Project investment information available on demand
- Common objectives and metrics defined for portfolio decision-making and analysis
- Strategic criteria used to maximize portfolio value

LEVEL 5
Optimizing Process

- Focus on continuous improvement of portfolio management processes

Integrating Project, Resource, Asset, and Product Portfolios

When you consider that the Project Management Institute defines a project as "a temporary endeavor undertaken to create a unique product, service or result,"[*] it is by definition understood that something new will exist within the organization at the completion of every project. It is also understood that every project consumes resources to create its product, service, or result. In order for those organizations at the highest levels of organizational maturity to operate as efficiently and effectively as possible, it is important to create a culture of governance that integrates the planning, consumption and creation of all organizational assets.

Those projects that create products, services or results add something new to the product or asset portfolios. Projects focused on enhancing existing products may not create additions to the portfolio but may change the attributes of certain products, affecting the overall value of the product portfolio. In all cases, however, resources and assets will be consumed by the projects to create the product of the project. Strategically planning the consumption of those resources enables an organization to do the right projects at the right time.

Managing the resources and assets being consumed by projects is just as important as managing project

[*] *A Guide to the Project Management Body of Knowledge, Third Edition,* Project Management Institute, 2004.

outcomes. Mature prioritization processes are key to keeping
all the cylinders firing in the right order at the right time.
Efficiency and effectiveness comes from an organization's
ability to know what portfolios exist, their relationship to
each other, their prioritization schemes and the optimal
performance of all the portfolios to ensure the highest levels
of productivity for the organization.

In many, or most, organizational cultures this is a
tremendous undertaking and requires a multi-phase
approach to achieve. The critical nature of understanding
the project portfolio management maturity of one's
organization establishes the starting point at which the
process maturity program begins and the development and
integration of all the portfolios within the organization.

Summary Description of Maturity Levels

THE PM Solutions' Project Portfolio Management Maturity Model features a staged representation of practices and processes that progress through a proven path of five successive levels, each serving as a foundation for the next.

Level 1: Initial Process

Although there is a recognition that there are project portfolio management processes, there are no established practices or standards, and individual project managers are not held to specific accountability by any process standards. Documentation is loose and ad hoc. Projects are funded despite absence of critical information that demonstrates expected and achieved improvements in program, business, or mission performance.

Level 2: Structured Process and Standards

Project portfolio management processes exist in the organization, but they are not considered an organizational standard. Documentation exists on these basic processes. Management supports the implementation of project portfolio management, but there is neither consistent understanding, involvement, nor organizational mandate to comply for all projects or project portfolios. Business value and prioritization levels are reviewed at the divisional level for larger, more visible projects. Information available for managing the project portfolio is often a mix between summary-level data and detail-level data.

Level 3: Organizational Standards and Institutionalized Process

All project portfolio management processes are in place and established as organizational standards. Nearly all projects and project portfolios use these processes with minimal exception — management has institutionalized the processes and standards with formal documentation existing on all processes and standards. Senior management is regularly involved in input and approval of key decisions and documents and in key project portfolio issues. The project portfolio management processes are typically automated. Each project and project portfolio is evaluated and managed in light of organizational strategy and business value.

Level 4: Managed Process

Project portfolios are managed with consideration as to how the portfolio performed in the past and what is expected for the future. Common objectives and metrics are defined for the portfolio and reviewed periodically with senior management to maintain/balance the portfolio. Project portfolio information is integrated with other corporate systems to optimize business decisions. Senior management clearly understands its role in the project portfolio management process and executes it well, managing at the right level, and clearly differentiating management styles and project portfolio management requirements for different sizes/complexities of projects and project portfolios. Project portfolio management processes, standards, and supporting systems are integrated with other corporate processes and systems.

Level 5: Optimizing Process

Processes are in place and actively used to improve project portfolio management activities. Lessons learned are regularly examined and used to improve project portfolio management processes, standards, and documentation. Management and the organization are focused not only on effectively managing project portfolios but also on continuous improvement. The metrics collected during execution are used not only to understand the performance of projects and project portfolios but also for improving management decision-making capability for the future.

Project Portfolio Management Maturity Model

Portfolio Governance

Portfolio governance addresses the organizational and decision-making processes used to manage and review the portfolio of projects. It includes establishing and maintaining the structure and procedures, and conducting the on-going assessment and improvement of the portfolio. The portfolio governance component ensures that the projects undertaken by the organization are aligned with its vision, strategy, and objectives.

Level 1

- There is no portfolio governance process in place.
- The evaluation of projects does not consider alignment with the organization's vision, strategy, or objectives.

Level 2

- There is a process for creating and defining division portfolio review boards.
- Each portfolio review board is created and defined with board membership integrating both project management and business knowledge.
- Each portfolio review board operates according to written policies and procedures in the organization-specific project portfolio management process guide.
- Each project investment or proposal is considered by a portfolio review board based upon the alignment criteria.
- Strategic alignment may be considered in the evaluation of projects, but no strategic criteria have been developed.

Level 3

- Division portfolio review boards consolidate and report to an enterprise-wide portfolio review board.

- Criteria for aligning project investment decision-making authority are established and maintained.

- Specific strategic criteria, such as alignment with business strategy, customer need and satisfaction, and competitive advantage have been developed, and projects are evaluated against these criteria to establish their acceptance in the portfolio.

Level 4

- Enterprise portfolio review board integrates lessons learned and processes portfolio status into current and future management project decision-making.

- Strategic criteria are being used to both accept the projects into the portfolio and in prioritizing the projects.

- Consideration is given to the various combinations of projects to maximize the value of the projects in relation to the strategic criteria.

- Project review boards review the fit of each project and combination of projects at each project review board meeting to ensure that any changes in vision, strategy, or objectives are evaluated with regard to the portfolio.

Level 5

- There is a process used to exploit management decision making to improve the value of project portfolio governance processes.

- Baseline data are collected for the organization's project portfolio governance processes.

- External comparable best-in-class project portfolio governance processes are identified and benchmarked.

• Improvements are made to the organization's project portfolio governance processes.

Project Opportunity Assessment

Project opportunity assessment focuses on the processes for identifying business needs that may be satisfied through the development of a solution(s) achieved by a project or projects. It includes processes and procedures for understanding and defining high-level business needs, crafting potential solution concepts, and harnessing the organizational resources to articulate these concepts as suggested projects.

Level 1

• Ad hoc or no standard process exists for identifying project opportunities or initiating projects.
• Roles and responsibilities are not aligned with identifying and managing project opportunities.
• A list of project opportunities is not available or maintained.
• Ad hoc or no processes are used for establishing the business value of projects.

Level 2

• Basic processes exist for identifying project opportunities.
• Roles and responsibilities for identifying project opportunities and initiating projects are defined.
• A project request form, project charter, or equivalent is used to identify and initiate projects.
• Key stakeholders and near-term business needs have been designated for each project.

- The Project Manager communicates with each of the key stakeholders using the standard, periodic reports.

Level 3

- A documented, organization-wide process is used for identifying and tracking project opportunities.
- Formal communication is provided back to each requester identifying the current status of a project opportunity or initiated project.
- An organization-wide process and documents are used to define business value of a project. The process includes a standard business case that is integrated with project management processes, financial and accounting practices, and other business processes.
- Roles and responsibilities are clearly defined for establishing business value.
- A formal project initiation process is used and maintained by the enterprise. Included in the project initiation process are formal approval processes.
- There is a process for examining the fundamental cost, benefit, schedule, and risk characteristics of each project before they are funded and combined with other projects into a portfolio.
- Each portfolio review board ensures that the cost-benefit-schedule-risk data and other required data are validated for each project within its span of control.

Level 4

- There is a process for conducting post-implementation reviews to learn from past projects and initiatives by comparing actual results to estimates.

- A portfolio review board identifies the projects for which a post-implementation review will be conducted and a post-implementation review is initiated for each designated project.

- Quantitative and qualitative project data are collected, evaluated for reliability, and analyzed during the post-implementation review.

- Lessons learned and improvement recommendations about the investment process and the individual investment are developed, captured in a written product or knowledge base, and distributed to decision makers.

- Project opportunity information is available by search criteria in an enterprise portfolio repository.

Level 5

- There is a process used to exploit management decision making to improve the value of project opportunity assessment processes.

- Baseline data are collected for the organization's project opportunity assessment processes.

- External comparable best-in-class project opportunity assessment processes are identified and benchmarked.

- Improvements are made to the organization's project opportunity assessment processes.

Project Prioritization and Selection

Project prioritization and selection addresses processes that help organizations review potential projects, prioritize these candidates based on sound decision-making criteria, and select the ones that provide the optimum value to the organization within its given resource constraints. It links prioritization and the selection of projects to the organizational strategies, and establishes a framework for systematically evaluating the business value of all projects, and the project portfolio in total.

Level 1

- Ad hoc or no processes are used for prioritizing potential and active work.
- Projects are funded despite absence of critical information that demonstrates expected and achieved improvements in program, business, or mission performance.

Level 2

- A standard process at the organization level exists for defining business value. The process includes the development of a business case (or equivalent document) whose detail may be proportionate to the level of investment.
- Roles and responsibilities are defined for establishing business value.
- Potential and active projects are prioritized using a simple prioritization scheme (1, 2, 3, etc.) and sorted at the organizational level.
- Prioritization may also be applied to different project categories.
- The prioritization scheme is based on high-level subjective factors.
- Business value and prioritization levels are reviewed by management, sponsor, and other related stakeholders.

Level 3

- Roles and responsibilities are clearly defined for prioritizing the portfolio of projects.

- A flexible prioritization scheme exists for ranking the portfolio of work based on agreed upon criteria. The prioritization scheme is supportive in aligning project strategy with business strategy and business unit/functional goals.

- The organization uses a structured process to develop new project proposals.

- Executives analyze and prioritize new project proposals according to established selection criteria.

- Executives make funding decisions for new project proposals according to an established process.

- Division portfolio review boards assess each of their project investments with respect to the project portfolio selection criteria.

- Each division portfolio review board prioritizes its portfolio of project investments using the portfolio selection criteria.

Level 4

- Standard models/business prioritization processes are used by management to prioritize projects/work at different levels within the enterprise.

- Standard models/business prioritization processes are validated by analyzing historical benefit/cost information and revised as required.

- A process exists for periodically updating the prioritization scores and business value of the portfolio of work.

- There is a process used by decision makers to create and communicate to the organization the criteria used to select and fund projects.
- The enterprise portfolio review board approves the core project portfolio selection criteria, including cost-benefit-schedule-risk criteria, based on the organization's mission, goals, strategies, and priorities.
- The project portfolio selection criteria are distributed throughout the organization.
- The project portfolio selection criteria are reviewed using cumulative experience and event-driven data and modified, as appropriate.
- There is a process for comparing worthwhile projects and then combining selected projects into a funded enterprise-wide portfolio.
- The portfolio review board assigns project proposals to a portfolio category.
- The portfolio review board examines the mix of proposals and projects across the common portfolio categories and makes selections for funding.
- The portfolio review board approves or modifies the annual cost-benefit-schedule-risk expectations for each of its selected project investments.
- A repository of portfolio development information is established, updated, and maintained.

Level 5

- There is a process used to exploit management decision making to improve the value of project prioritization and selection processes.
- Baseline data are collected for the organization's project prioritization and selection processes.

- External comparable best-in-class project prioritization and selection processes are identified and benchmarked.
- Improvements are made to the organization's project prioritization and selection processes.

Portfolio and Project Communications Management

Portfolio and project communications management deals with the processes for collecting and sharing information on each project in the portfolio, and summarizing this information in a manner that enables the organization to make strategic portfolio decisions. When properly executed, portfolio and project communications management helps the organization make rational and unbiased decisions, with full knowledge of each projects' value to the portfolio, and balance this projected value with resource constraints.

Level 1

- There is no acknowledged division or organization-wide portfolio with a list of approved projects.
- Portfolio-based information (e.g. status, project categories, etc.) is not defined.
- Portfolio information is not readily available and/or not communicated to the organization.

Level 2

- A list of active and pending projects is maintained for each division and is updated periodically.
- A defined process and cycle is used for reviewing and updating the portfolio of projects within each division.
- Cross-divisional projects apply project management processes according to corporate standards.

- Project status is communicated to the division that has responsibility for the project.
- Each project contains: descriptive information; owner and sponsor information; timing and estimated resources; and high-level status information (e.g. potential, active, hold, cancelled, completed, next milestone, etc.).
- Each project is categorized to ensure that investments are balanced to meet the enterprise's goals and objectives (e.g., by program, functional area, strategic vs. tactical, etc.).
- A basic process exists for aggregating project data to build a portfolio "snapshot" for the division.
- Portfolio information is communicated across and down the division through meetings and other communication processes.

Level 3

- A process exists for aggregating portfolio-level information to the business unit (or organizational level) for review and evaluation of impact to investment balance.
- Detailed information is tracked for each project. Information should include descriptive and performance information, resource estimates (high-level), business value, status, project categorization, and cost and schedule information.
- Risk information may also be tracked for each project/ work opportunity.
- A project list/database is maintained accounting for new projects, completed projects, and changes to the project portfolio organization-wide.
- Organization-wide projects are conducted with standardized project management processes and stakeholders work together in a collaborative fashion both

in terms of accomplishing the current project objectives and anticipating future project and portfolio requirements.

Level 4

- Project portfolio information is audited to validate the data and assumptions.
- The organization's asset inventory is developed and maintained according to a written procedure, including changes.
- Project investment information is available on demand to decision makers and other affected parties.
- Historical asset inventory records are maintained for future selections and assessments.

Level 5

- There is a process used to exploit management decision making to improve the value of portfolio and project communications management processes.
- Baseline data are collected for the organization's portfolio and project communications management processes.
- External comparable best-in-class portfolio and project communications management processes are identified and benchmarked.
- Improvements are made to the organization's portfolio and project communications management processes.

Portfolio Performance Management

Portfolio performance management allows the organization to evaluate the performance of the portfolio of projects and their relative value to the organization. It allows management to evaluate the portfolio of projects, analyze different portfolio scenarios, and re-plan for changes in strategy or financial budgets. This includes evaluating the business value actually realized by each project, program, or initiative; and using that information for repositioning the organization's project portfolio.

Level 1

- Ad hoc or no standard process exists for managing the current portfolio of projects.
- Ad hoc or no standard processes are used for reviewing the portfolio with the sponsor organization.
- Project reviews of high-risk/high-value projects are not conducted.
- Portfolio management controls are unstructured, ill-timed, and inconsistent. Management rarely reviews project performance data.
- Organization rarely has an up-to-date and complete inventory of assets.
- Organization rarely evaluates project outcomes or identifies lessons learned.

Level 2

- Portfolio information is reviewed periodically with the sponsor organization.
- A defined process is used for analyzing and reporting on the portfolio, including reporting tools (graphs, charts, presentations, etc.). The process involves multiple levels within the organization including senior management, steering committees, project management office, and other stakeholders.
- High- risk/high-value projects are easily identified and typically conduct project reviews to apprise executive management of current issues.

- There is a project oversight process in which the organization monitors all projects relative to cost and schedule expectations.
- Each project's up-to-date cost and schedule data are provided to the appropriate portfolio review board.
- Using established criteria, the portfolio review board oversees each project's performance on a periodic basis by comparing actual cost and schedule data to expectations.
- The portfolio review board directs special reviews of projects that have not met predetermined performance standards.
- The portfolio review board ensures that corrective actions were developed and tracked.

Level 3

- Organizational standards and institutionalized processes exist for analyzing and reporting on the enterprise portfolio (roll-up includes business units, functional units, project categories, etc.).
- The portfolio is actively analyzed (using varied views) and used in making balanced investment.
- Organizational standards involve the use of consistent data fields, common definitions, and standard business rules.
- There is a process that builds upon the project oversight process by adding the elements of project benefit and risk management to the control process activities.
- An organization-wide portfolio review board monitors the performance of the projects in the portfolio by comparing actual cost-benefit-schedule-risk data to expectations.
- Using established criteria, the portfolio review board identifies its projects that have not met predetermined cost-benefit-schedule-risk performance expectations.

- The portfolio review board ensures that project managers develop an action plan to apply the corrective actions identified.
- All projects conduct project reviews to apprise management of current issues.

Level 4

- Common objectives and metrics are defined for the portfolio of work and reviewed periodically with management to maintain/balance the portfolio of projects.
- Portfolio analysis using standard metrics is integrated into management's decision processes.
- There is a process for evaluating portfolio performance and using this information to improve both current project portfolio management processes and future portfolio performance.
- Comprehensive project portfolio performance measurement data are defined and collected using agreed upon methods.
- There is a process for analyzing and managing the succession of identified project investments and assets to their higher-value successors.
- The portfolio review board develops criteria for identifying project investments that may meet succession status.

Level 5

- There is a process used to exploit management decision making to improve the value of project portfolio performance management processes.
- Baseline data are collected for the organization's project portfolio performance management processes.
- External comparable best-in-class project portfolio performance management processes are identified and benchmarked.

- Improvements are made to the organization's project portfolio performance management processes.
- Reports are developed on trends at all levels of the organization's portfolio. Aggregate performance data trends are analyzed.
- Portfolio process and portfolio improvement recommendations are developed and implemented.
- Project investments are periodically analyzed for succession and appropriate investments are identified as succession candidates.
- The interdependency of each investment with other investments in the project portfolio is analyzed.
- The portfolio review board makes a succession decision for each candidate project investment.

Portfolio Resource Management

Portfolio resource management includes the processes that allow an organization to effectively assign the appropriate resources (number and skills) to successfully execute the projects in the portfolio. It helps to ensure that the organization's resources (typically people and time) are allocated properly to meet the business needs. It also provides management with information for forecasting future resource requirements.

Level 1

- Resources are assigned to projects on an availability basis using ad hoc processes.

Level 2

- Resources are identified according to their skill set and availability.
- Each division has captured the skill sets of its resources and manages their time availability in a collaborative fashion for project matrix management.
- Project prioritization is established at division-level, but there are guidelines for managing project priorities with limited resources in a cross-divisional and collaborative fashion.

Level 3

- A resource-pool management process exists that captures skills sets, availability and knowledge management across the organization.
- Project priorities are established from the enterprise portfolio review board and division leaders are expected to optimally assign resources based upon resource skills, prioritization, and established project priorities.
- Resources other than people are also contained in the overall resource pool. Equipment, hardware, software licenses, specialty teams (such as testing) are included in this category to ensure that all constraints are tracked.

Level 4

- Enterprise and division resource analysis and reporting occurs on a scheduled basis to ensure that the organization maximizes its potential productivity and effectiveness in realizing the objectives of the projects and financial drivers for the portfolio.

Level 5

- There is a process used to exploit management decision making to improve the value of project portfolio resource management processes.
- Baseline data are collected for the organization's project portfolio resource management processes.
- External comparable best-in-class project portfolio resource management processes are identified and benchmarked.
- Improvements are made to the organization's project portfolio resource management processes.

INDEX